BE HEALED

Racial   – Economic
          – Education
          – Healthcare
          – Criminal Justice
          – Housing

"*Be Healed* is a compilation of testimonies and a guide that allows one to fully embrace the love poured out through the Holy Spirit in generating charisms for the Church. Schuchts has given us a simple and profound gift of Jesus' healing ministry and our call to continue it."

Jane Guenther
Coordinator of Catholic Renewal Center in St. Louis

"This is a great book and really enjoyable reading. If you have struggled with physical and emotional issues, this book is for you. *Be Healed* will build hope and expectation that you can receive your healing. It takes a balanced approach to healing in Christ for the whole person and how you can live life to the fullest."

Gary Oates
Author of *Open My Eyes, Lord*

"*Be Healed* is an invitation to encounter the Lord as your healer. Bob Schuchts writes with humility and compassion, imparting wisdom gained from a lifetime of discovery of what it means to be whole in Christ and how to invite others to receive God's healing presence. *Be Healed* will impart wisdom through real-life stories, personal journeys, and penetrating scriptural stories, all in an authentic Catholic context. It will open doors for you to look at life from the view of the Lord's passion to see you liberated from those things that hold you back from being the person you were created to be."

Neal Lozano
Author of *Unbound*

"*Be Healed* will bring you into a deeper encounter with the Trinity and a new openness and freedom in every area of your life."

From the foreword by Rev. Mark Toups
Vicar general of the Diocese of Houma–Thibodaux

"Quite simply, this is one of the most important books I've ever read. It opened my heart and mind to my wounds, and to Jesus' desire to heal them. I cannot recommend this book enough to every single person who walks the earth."

Patrick Lencioni
New York Times best-selling author of *The Five Dysfunctions of a Team*
Founder, The Amazing Parish

"In *Be Healed*, Bob Schuchts takes the reader into the life of a changed man, sharing the story of how he received spiritual, psychological, and emotional healing. Our world, filled with brokenness and suffering, needs to experience the truth of Christ's healing power! Reading this book will help you begin that encounter with Jesus."

Most Reverend Samuel J. Aquila
Archbishop of Denver

"This book deeply touched my heart and opened new levels of healing in my life. Whether you are just beginning your healing journey or have been walking this path for years, *Be Healed* will encourage, enlighten, challenge, and transform you in your encounter with Jesus Christ. I highly recommend it."

Sr. Miriam James Heidland, S.O.L.T
Author of *Loved as I Am*

"Schuchts profoundly understands the human heart, its self-protective tendencies, and its need for healing. By sharing insights gleaned from both his own experience of woundedness and healing and from his many years of professional counseling and prayer with others, he helps readers open themselves to the healing Jesus offers. A potentially life-changing book."

Peter F. Ryan, S.J.
Theology professor at Sacred Heart Major Seminary

BE HEALED

A Guide to Encountering the Powerful Love of Jesus in Your Life

BOB SCHUCHTS

AVE MARIA PRESS AVE Notre Dame, Indiana

Nihil Obstat: Héctor R.G. Pérez y Robles, S.T.D.
                   Censor Librorum

Imprimatur: + Gregory L. Parkes, D.D., J.C.L.
                   Bishop of Pensacola–Tallahassee

Founded in 1865, Ave Maria Press is a ministry of the United States Province of Holy Cross.

www.avemariapress.com

Paperback ISBN-13 978-1-59471-476-4

E-book ISBN-13 978-1-59471-477-1

Cover image © Thinkstock.com

Cover and text design by Brian C. Conley.

Printed and bound in the United States of America.

Library of Congress Cataloging-in-Publication Data
Schuchts, Bob.
Be healed : a guide to encountering the powerful love of Jesus in your life / Bob Schuchts.
    pages cm
Includes bibliographical references.
ISBN 1-59471-476-2 (978-1-59471-476-4)
1. God (Christianity)--Love. 2. Healing--Religious aspects--Catholic Church. 3. Forgive-ness--Religious aspects--Catholic Church. 4. Forgiveness of sin. 5. Catholic Church--Doctrines. I. Title.
BT140.S37 2014
203'.1--dc23

                   2013044587

CONTENTS

FOREWORD

I first met Bob Schuchts in October 2004 at a men's conference in Houma, Louisiana, three years after being ordained to the Catholic priesthood. At that time I had already heard thousands of confessions and spent countless hours listening to others as a spiritual director. Still growing in my familiarity in the spiritual life, I knew God's desire for our freedom was infinitely greater than our own; however, I had far too often felt that there was indeed something missing.

As the men's conference unfolded, I began to listen to penitents express sin, and the full nature thereof, as never before. Thus, the penitents were disposed to receive the grace of the sacrament from the depths of their being. I witnessed transformation before me and knew this was how the sacraments were meant to be received. Naturally, I asked how this was. What was happening? The Lord soon led me to a conference room where Bob was ministering to a small group of men.[1] As he finished his individual ministry, he encouraged the men to bring their hearts to the sacraments, specifically the Sacrament of Reconciliation. Aha. This was what was happening. Men were experiencing the Lord in the midst of their wounds; thus, they were more disposed to the confessions that I eventually heard.

Since 2004 I have had the privilege of growing in my relationship with Bob. I have benefited from his ministry one on one, as the Lord brought further healing and freedom in my own heart. I have ministered with him at conferences, as well as in individual inner healing prayer. Finally, I have enjoyed a personal friendship, celebrating our journey together as we both walk with the Lord.

Amidst all of the things that we have done together, I am most grateful for Bob's ministry to the seminarians and priests of the Diocese of Houma–Thibodaux, Louisiana, as well as other dioceses across the United States and Canada. The Lord longs for the renewal of his Church, and this renewal must begin with the renewal of the priesthood. With that goal in mind, the Diocese of Houma–Thibodaux, under the leadership of Bishop Sam Jacobs, in 2005 introduced a special year of spiritual formation for all seminarians, following their completion of philosophy and preceding their study of theology. The design of the spiritual year is to strengthen the seminarian's capacity to "live in intimate and unceasing union with the Trinity" and to form priests who are "mature, viral, and capable of cultivating an authentic spiritual paternity."[2]

Pope Benedict XVI said, "The faithful expect only one thing from priests: that they be specialists in promoting the encounter between man and God." For this to happen, "priests need to be honest with themselves, open with their spiritual director and trusting in divine mercy."[3] Bob has been essential in assisting our seminarians and priests as they grow in honesty with themselves and in learning to trust in divine mercy in the depths of their heart. In fact, as I reminisce with the seminarians and priests about their priestly formation, Bob is most often mentioned as one the most influential persons in their entire formation.

One by one, as these young men are ordained to the priesthood of Jesus Christ, they are more confident in their spiritual paternity and their ability to lead their parishioners into an encounter with Christ. They also understand in the depths of their hearts what Pope Benedict XVI meant when he said that "healing is an essential part . . . of Christianity."[4] Healing, transformation, and a new life in Christ are indeed possible and necessary for the entire people of God.

Unfortunately, far too many doubt the power and desire of the Lord to bring this healing. As Christopher West has noted, "Christ's people tend to accept discord . . . 'as just the way it is' . . . without reference to God's original plan and its hope for restoration in Christ."[5] Most live life with flat tires and think this is as good as it gets. The unexpressed grief in our hearts traps us in our own prison. We need to be set free.

The good news of the Gospel is, "What came to be through him was life, and this life was the light of the human race; the light shines in the darkness, and the darkness has not overcome it" (Jn 1:3b–5). God desires us. He desires all of us: all of our hearts, all of our lives, and all of our history. Where we experience darkness, he desires light. Where we experience un-freedom, he desires freedom. I pray that the Lord continues to bless the ministry of healing in the Church, in all its many forms, and those who pilgrim through this book. May your journey bring you into a deeper encounter with the Trinity and a new openness and freedom in every area of your life.

Rev. Mark Toups

INTRODUCTION

[Jesus'] gaze, the touch of his heart heals us . . . enabling us to become truly ourselves and thus totally of God.

Pope Benedict XVI,
Saved by Hope

Somewhere deep inside each one of us is a burning desire to finally become the person God created us to be. Yearning to be fully alive, we long to give ourselves as a gift wholeheartedly back to God. Yet despite these stirrings, many of us hesitate and resist, fearing the very thing we desire. While we long to be made pure and whole, we avoid God's process of purification and healing.

I wonder if the Samaritan woman felt a similar reluctance before encountering Jesus at Jacob's well (see Jn 4). Do you remember her story? Her brief but powerful encounter with Jesus exposed the secrets of her heart and set her free to love again. She came to the well with an insatiable *thirst*. Her many worldly lovers had left these cravings for love unfulfilled. Neither could she satisfy their consuming appetites. One by one, they had thrown her away like a day-old beverage that had lost its taste. We can only imagine how hopeless and unworthy she felt before her encounter with Jesus. Consider her shock when Jesus approached her, asking her for water.

1

According to the customs of the time, a Samaritan woman would not be permitted to speak with a Jewish man. Furthermore, some scholars suggest she came this late in the day to avoid facing the people in her own village. But Jesus was not a bit surprised by their encounter. Coming to the well, Jesus too was *thirsty*, though he was seeking more than water. He thirsted for this woman, with a deep desire that was totally different from the way the other men desired her. While they sought to consume her for their own pleasure, Jesus longed to satisfy her thirst by pouring himself out on her behalf. He desired to fulfill her, not to use her.

Can you picture the scene as they greet each other and his gentle gaze meets hers? I envision her immediately avoiding eye contact with Jesus. But then sensing something unusual in his presence, I imagine her looking up, being drawn into Jesus' penetrating gaze. Piercing her shame and reaching to the depths of her soul with his words, he *sees her* and speaks to her heart as no one has ever done before now. His searing love purifies her heart, burning away the shame-based lies that have tarnished her self-respect. Her previously unreachable well, the well of her soul, is now overflowing with living water. Running into the village, she longs to offer a refreshing drink to everyone she meets. She is radically transformed by her encounter with Jesus. Seeing her own dignity for the first time, she now desires to give herself completely to God. She wants to tell everyone about this man who "knew everything" about her. She invites all of us to come and meet him for ourselves.

This kind of radical transformation is not just a nice story out of the Bible. Jesus offers the same kind of healing for each one of us today. I have witnessed similar kinds of transformation in our Healing the Whole Person conferences. The people who come and encounter Jesus' powerful love can't wait to tell many others. These conferences were originally developed in cooperation with Father Mark Toups as an intensive week of human formation and training for the seminarians of his diocese. In time they have expanded to include participants from all over North America, including priests, religious, and lay people of all ages and vocations, and pastors and leaders from across the Body of Christ. We now believe it is time to share these treasured graces with a larger audience, in order to invite you to encounter the powerful love of Jesus in your life.

I encourage you to take an honest look inside yourself, as we embark on this journey of healing together. Are you thirsting for more? Do you long to be more fully alive but find yourself restricted by fear, shame, and disillusionment? Have you tried to fill empty spaces in your heart with unholy relationships or activities that never really satisfy? If so, this book is for you.

In the same way, if you are in a ministry where you desire to help others find greater freedom and healing in their life, I believe you will find much in this book that will benefit you greatly, but first I urge you to apply the material to your own life. Whether we realize it or not we are each wounded and in need of healing. I was involved in ministry for years before I saw my own real and deep need for healing. Now I realize that my healing process is never ending and ever deepening. Jesus meets us time and again, as he did the Samaritan woman, in the place of our deepest thirst.

Jesus brought healing to the Samaritan woman with majestic simplicity. He invited her into an encounter with himself; he revealed her brokenness; and he gave her the finest medicine—his love and truth—to heal her wounds. Jesus often heals each of us in the same simple way. For that reason I have chosen to organize the book into these three overall parts, depicting the three stages of the healing process: part 1, Encountering Jesus (chapters 1–4), part 2, Facing Our Brokenness (chapters 5–7), and part 3, Healing Our Wounds (chapters 8–10).

The intention is to guide you into your own healing encounter with Jesus. To support that objective, I have been careful to ground the teaching in biblical truth, in keeping with the two-thousand-year-old healing tradition of the Church. Within each chapter you will find references from scripture and from various Christian authors involved in the healing ministry. The title, *Be Healed*, is based in the belief that Jesus' fundamental mission is to restore us to wholeness (see Lk 4:18–19; 1 Thes 5:23). Healing any part of us by necessity influences our entire being (*CCC*, 363–68). Whether we realize it or not, our physical illnesses, spiritual afflictions, and psychological infirmities are profoundly intertwined.

Throughout the book you will find engaging and at times amazing stories of personal healing experiences that illustrate this interconnection. Some of these come from my personal life and family. Others are drawn from the lives of people with whom I have had the privilege to pray with over the years. I trust that you will find aspects of your own story or ministry in several of these accounts.

To aid you in applying the teaching and stories to your own life, I have included various figures and tables to summarize teaching points in several of the chapters. To that same end, questions for personal reflection are offered in each chapter. For those who want to go deeper with this material, we also offer workbooks, CDs, and other resources through the *John Paul II Healing Center* at JPIIhealingcenter.org. Please contact us directly for those additional materials and for information about our conferences.

As you prepare to begin this journey, I invite you to read with the eyes of your heart as well as with your physical eyes. You may find it beneficial to read through the entire book the first time to gain a general understanding of the material. Then, on the second time through, I encourage you to read slowly and deliberately, praying as you go. Questions for personal reflection are offered throughout each chapter, and in the conclusion. For those who want to engage more fully in this process, I encourage you to form a small support group with a trusted community to go through these questions together. If you would like additional resources, we offer workbooks and CDs through the John Paul II Healing Center. You may contact us directly at jpiihealingcenter.org for these materials.

PART ONE
ENCOUNTERING JESUS

I worry some of you still have not really met Jesus—one to one—you and Jesus alone. . . . He loves you, but even more—He longs for you.

Blessed Mother Teresa of Calcutta,
Letter to the Missionaries of Charity Family

CHAPTER ONE

DO YOU WANT
TO BE HEALED?

*Healing is an essential dimension of . . . Christianity. . . .
It expresses the entire content of our redemption.*

Pope Benedict XVI,
Jesus of Nazareth

I am in awe at Jesus' insight into human nature. I know he created us, but still his ability to see right into the heart of a situation always amazes me. No matter how badly bound we are, he seems to know the exact key to unlock our prison doors. Time and again throughout the gospels, we see his wisdom manifested in his interaction with each person he meets. His encounter with the man at the pool of Bethesda is a prime example (Jn. 5:1–9).

Can you fathom what it was like for this lame man to lay beside a "healing" pool for thirty-eight years but never get in? To put it into a modernday context, imagine someone lying beside the healing waters of Lourdes for thirty-eight years. Can you even imagine that? Day after day, year after year, this man of Bethesda waited helplessly for someone to assist him. Thousands passed him by until Jesus stopped and listened to the cry of his heart.

I'm sure Jesus approached this poor man with compassion, but I must admit I'm a bit troubled by his opening words: "Do you want to be well?" (Jn 5:6). To me, it sounds like Jesus is accusing the man of playing the victim. My initial reaction is to step in to defend this helpless man: *Of course he wants to be healed. Look how long he has been suffering.* But then, coming to my senses, I realize this is Jesus whom I am questioning. He must know something about the deeper paralysis of this man's soul that isn't immediately obvious to me. After all these years, it appears this lame man has given up hope that he will ever be healed. Who could blame him? Why hold on to hope, only to be disappointed again and again?

The longer I ponder Jesus' question to this man, the more I begin to feel a bit uneasy myself. He is not just asking this lame man if he wants to be healed. His question is directed to me and to you as well. After all these years of struggling with our various physical, psychological, and spiritual infirmities, have we somehow resigned ourselves to our broken condition, believing "this is as good as life gets"? Have we also given in to hopelessness, believing we won't be healed? Most of the time, we aren't even conscious of our resignation. We just accept our condition and bear it as best we can. Can you relate?

TAKE A MOMENT

Take a moment to examine your readiness for Jesus to heal you.

- Do you recognize your need for healing? *No*
- Do you want to be healed? *I dont Know*
- Have you given up hope that you can be healed?
- Do you believe Jesus desires to heal you? *Yes*
- What attitudes of doubt and unbelief stand in the way of you receiving Jesus' powerful healing love? *Dont feel I need healing??*

You may be wondering what I mean when I use the term *healing* throughout this book. Simply stated, healing is the process of being made whole: body, soul, and spirit. It includes the restoration of our communion with God, our own integration, and reconciliation with those around us. This is consistent with most dictionary definitions, including the following from *Merriam Webster's*:

1. to make sound or whole <heal a wound>, to restore to health
2. to cause (an undesirable condition) to be overcome . . . to patch up (a breach or division) <heal a breach between friends>
3. to restore to original purity or integrity <healed of sin>

These definitions are reflective of the way the word *healing* is used throughout the scriptures: to save, to cure, to make whole, to repair a breach, to restore communion, to give a therapeutic remedy, and so forth. The lame man of Bethesda's most obvious need was for physical healing, but Jesus saw that he needed a much deeper healing. Before losing hope, he had a natural and God-given desire to be made whole and to have all his relationships restored. Though paralyzed with hopelessness, he could still acknowledge these buried desires.

No matter how much we have suppressed our desires, you and I also have a deep yearning to be healed. Why else do we go to doctors, dentists, therapists, priests, and ministers? Why else do so many people spend a significant portion of their time, money, and energy in the pursuit of health and wholeness? According to the World Bank, health care currently consumes anywhere from 10 to 20 percent of our resources.[1]

We pursue health and wholeness because God has built the desire for healing into the fabric of every human being. As Pope Benedict attests, healing is essential to our Christian faith. As Christians, we believe that Jesus came to earth for this purpose—to restore us to wholeness and to bring us back into full communion with the Father and each other.

$$\maltese$$

This faith, revealed in sacred scriptures, has been faithfully proclaimed by the Church for two thousand years: "'Heal the sick'! The Church has received this charge from the Lord and strives to carry it out. . . . She believes in the life-giving presence of Christ, the physician of souls and bodies" (*CCC*, 1509). Stop a minute and let those time-tested words sink in. Jesus, the incarnation of God our Healer, is the ultimate physician of our souls and bodies (Ex 15:25–26). He not only forgives all our sins, but he also heals all our diseases, according the Psalmist (Ps 103:3).

Jesus' healing miracles, past and present, are expressions of the Father's tender compassion and intimate concern for each of us in our brokenness and suffering. They point to the ultimate healing he won for us on Calvary. Pope Benedict's assertion sums it all up: "Healing . . . expresses the *entire content* of our redemption."[2] For the past two thousand years of Church history, all our worship, all our theology, and all our prayers are directed toward our restoration, as we are brought ever deeper into communion with the Holy Trinity.

Healing is a process, which will be completely fulfilled in heaven. But the process must begin now in each of our lives, as we face our various physical ailments, psychological difficulties, and spiritual afflictions. So the question Jesus asked of the man of Bethesda is directed to each one of us, *"Do you want to be healed?"* In some ways, we all resemble the lame man lying near the healing waters. As close as Jesus is, we can't reach him by ourselves; we need his help. At the same time, Jesus will not heal us without our consent and cooperation. Many of us don't realize we even need healing, or how deeply we need it. We mistakenly believe we are fine just the way we are. I was that person in my twenties and early thirties. Like the religious leaders of Jesus' time, I thought I was fine and had no need of the Divine Physician (Mk 2:17). My pride blinded me, but Jesus opened my eyes to my tremendous need for healing.

As you hear my story, I pray you will be able to relate in some way. I have found that underlying our individual life circumstances, we all share a common brokenness. I hope that my experience will stir you to look at your own story and recognize your own brokenness. As you do, I pray you will encounter the powerful love of Jesus in your life like never before.

I am only half joking when I tell people that I began my career as a family therapist at the ripe old age of fourteen. I didn't actually earn my degree until the age of twenty-six, but by the time I finished my graduate training I had many years of informal experience "playing therapist" in my family of origin. Life circumstances thrust me into this role rather abruptly when my dad, an otherwise good and loving father, made some life-altering choices, which left me, my mom, and six siblings abandoned and left to fend for ourselves.

Dad's leaving broke my heart and devastated our entire family. Our once-secure world was shattered. Though all of us suffered enormously, the damage was most evident in my older brother Dave, who at sixteen found his solace in heroin. In 1969, he attended the infamous Woodstock gathering, grew his hair long, rebelled against authority, and found his identity in the emerging hippie subculture. Soon after dad left, Dave also left home. With their leaving, I lost my two closest friends and male role models. Watching them fall, I felt like one of the lemmings who stood in danger of being next over the cliff. I needed to do something to protect myself, my mom, and my younger brothers and sisters. As the second oldest, I took it upon myself to shoulder the emotional burdens of our large and distressed family. In the process, I denied my own pain and became overly concerned about everyone else's well-being.

Losing Dad and Dave was only the beginning of a very difficult eighth-grade year. Within the next twelve months I lost everything and everyone I loved, with the exception of my mom and other siblings. Dad's leaving seemed to remove a hedge of protection from around our family, and we became open prey to the enemy of our souls. Things got considerably worse, very quickly.

Within weeks of Dad leaving, my basketball coach of four years, who was also my science and homeroom teacher, invited four teammates and me on a camping trip. While there, he climbed into my bed in the middle of the night and tried to molest me. I am grateful that I woke up and got away, but the wounds of betrayal remained. That same weekend, my first girlfriend and several of my closest friends back home engaged in sexual intimacies with one another while I was gone.

Having already been betrayed by my dad and coach, I was reeling. Whom could I trust? There was more to come. Five months later, I became enamored with another beautiful girl and entrusted my heart to her. As Yogi Berra quipped, "It was déjà vu all over again." I went away to basketball camp for three weeks, and when I returned, I found out she too had been unfaithful. I learned not to trust my heart to anyone and concluded that going away to camp could be dangerous.

During all this time we didn't hear from Dad for over a year. I remember lying in bed at night wondering whether he was alive or dead. My brother Dave eventually found him in another city, where he had started a second family. This was the final blow. It seemed my entire foundation of trust was ripped out from under me—and not just from me but also from our entire family. In the wake of the public humiliation, Mom decided she needed to start over, prompting her to move us away from our childhood home in Bethel Park, a suburb of Pittsburgh.

In the middle of my ninth-grade year, we moved as a family to South Florida, leaving everyone and everything of value back home in Pennsylvania. I didn't want to move, but I had no choice. I loved Bethel Park, where I had lived all my life, and I detested everything about my new environment in South Florida. I realize that others have much more traumatic things to deal with in life, but for my short life, which until this point had been quite secure and happy, everything was turned upside down. Life was chaotic, and without my awareness, my trust in God was severely wounded.

In spite of all the upheaval, we managed to survive as a family, living on the Father's providence with a little help from food stamps. We each found our own unique ways to cope. After a year of struggle and feeling completely lost in the new environment, I began ex-celling again in school and sports. My role as "family therapist" for my mom and siblings also gave me a sense of purpose and meaning. Despite a few sports injuries and surgeries, I *thought* I was healthy.

At the time, I had no concept that my physical ailments might be pointing to underlying spiritual and psychological issues, which I hadn't faced. I managed to get all the way through high school, col-lege, graduate school, and then into my profession without dealing with my inner pain and brokenness. As far as I was concerned, the past was clearly in the rearview mirror and I never needed to revisit it. Have you ever felt that way? That your past is behind you and you don't need to look back? Sometimes we even misquote the Bible to justify our unwillingness to face our pain: "Forgetting what lies be-hind but straining forward to what lies ahead, I continue my pursuit toward the goal" (Phil 3:13b–14a).

I was tenaciously goal-driven, achieving enough to be accepted at Columbia University, where I played football for four years. From then on, I was completely focused on starting a family and establish-ing a career. Before finishing college, I married my girlfriend and best friend from high school, Margie O'Donnell. A year after getting married, we received the beautiful gift of our daughter Carrie, and then two years after that, while I was still in graduate school, we welcomed our second beautiful daughter, Kristen.

Upon completion of my doctorate, I established a private practice as a marriage and family therapist, where I continued to help others with *their* family problems. I also taught courses in marriage and family part-time at Florida State University, sharing all the wisdom I had learned to help *others* find true happiness. Do you hear the irony and pride?

On the home front, Margie and I were enjoying our precious daughters, and though we were struggling some as a couple, we were managing. Within a few years after graduation, we bought our first home in a cute neighborhood with a great elementary school. When it came time for Carrie and Kristen to enter school, Margie returned to nursing school to pursue her dream of becoming a labor and delivery nurse.

I wish you were either cold or hot. So, because you are lukewarm, neither hot nor cold, I will spit you out of my mouth. . . . Those whom I love, I reprove and chastise.

Revelation 3:15b–16, 19a

Despite all these outward accomplishments, I was feeling restless on the inside. Having been goal-driven with sports and school for so long, I didn't know how to handle the void that came after graduation. Though well-respected professionally and having a full life away from work, I couldn't shake this unsettled feeling. I had no idea what was missing, until one day my new neighbor invited me to a prayer breakfast and Bible study.

When I showed up at Shoney's restaurant the next week, the Holy Spirit wasted little time getting my attention. In our very first meeting together, one of the men read a passage from the book of

Revelation. As he read, I sensed Jesus speaking directly to me: "I wish you were either cold or hot. So, because you are lukewarm, neither hot nor cold, I will spit you out of my mouth. . . . Those whom I love, I reprove and chastise" (Rv 3:15b–16, 19a). Jesus' words startled me and I felt a conviction from the Holy Spirit as never before.

Without realizing it, I had been coasting in my spiritual life. Sitting on the proverbial fence, I had not fully given my heart to Jesus or anyone else for that matter. I was afraid of many things, but mostly I feared losing control and getting hurt again if I entrusted my heart to anyone. Unconsciously, I was still protecting myself from all that had happened nearly fifteen years earlier. Hidden terror, masked as emotional insulation, kept me from giving my heart completely to Margie. I feared she might reject me, leave me, or find someone else. Worse yet, my experience in college, where I had taken steps in faith, led me to believe that she would not like it if I gave my heart unreservedly to Jesus. Until this moment, I was able to live in the lukewarm middle. But with Jesus' rebuke, I felt as though I had to choose between Margie and him. Whichever way I chose, I feared the other one would reject me.

Looking back, I can see the goodness of Jesus' rebuke, as it served as a catalyst for me to face my wounded heart. At the time though, nothing about it seemed good. I only felt panic. Literally this confrontation with truth threw me into a panic attack, which simultaneously drove me into therapy for the first time in my life. I went from being the one who smugly helped others to realizing how much I desperately needed help myself.

Therapy was beneficial in encouraging me to face my hidden pain. I learned to express my emotions and discovered deep hurts that I had kept buried. I started to feel the relief of having someone who cared to listen to my needs. But after the first few months, therapy became threatening in a new way, as it stirred up issues between Margie and me. Without knowing it, I was projecting all my hurt and unhealed emotional wounds onto her. I was blind to her needs and angry that she wasn't meeting mine the way I thought she should.

When our therapist recommended we separate, I decided I was done with therapy. The thought of hurting Margie and our children the way I had been hurt was out of the question. My tightly wound self-sufficiency was quickly unraveling, and I didn't know what to do or where to turn. Though I couldn't see it at the time, the Holy Spirit was moving actively in my life, drawing me toward Jesus. After my prayer breakfast experience, I knew I needed to give my allegiance to Jesus, even if Margie was not okay with it. I was learning daily from studying the scriptures and praying earnestly for the first time in my adult life. I was going to church and beginning to discover Christian community. Attending "Marriage Encounter" and a "Life in the Spirit" brought some hope, but I was not able to let go of control enough to allow the Holy Spirit free access to my heart.

A major breakthrough came when our parish decided to begin a renewal program called Christ Renews His Parish (CRHP), a process of personal and community renewal that grew out of the Curcillo Movement in the Catholic Church. Mother Teresa once told Pope John Paul II that CRHP was one of several renewal processes that would transform the Church. It turned out to be life-changing for me, for our parish community, and eventually for nearly all the members of my family as well. I signed up for the first weekend with an unusual excitement. I now understand why. My life has never been the same since.

The first weekend was a nice change of pace, as I learned to receive rather than be the one responsible for meeting others' needs.

I discovered that other men shared my intense hunger for God. I was amazed and encouraged by the real sharing of these men of all ages. I had never experienced that kind of honesty and vulnerability with people at church before. Following an enjoyable but otherwise unspectacular weekend, we entered a time of formation together, learning to become disciples of Jesus. We practiced the art of spiritual discernment, listening to the Holy Spirit and to one another. The intimacy of genuine Christian community became a great balm after years of lone-ranger Christianity.

To this day, some of my closest friends came from that group of men. By the end of our formation period, we had become a unified team, ready to offer the gift of the weekend to a new group of men. We all experienced incredible joy serving in communion, discovering our unique gifts, and seeing how Jesus wove them together to personally meet the needs of the new attendees. As lay director, I was the primary leader on the team, serving under our pastor's authority. After years of ministering to others solo as a teacher and therapist, this corporate ministry was deeply satisfying. The heavy burden of feeling responsible for people's needs, which had become second nature since Dad left, lifted miraculously. Jesus was doing the heavy lifting, and we all felt privileged to be his co-laborers, shouldering his easy yoke (see Mt 11:20).

I could feel my heart coming alive in this environment of spiritual fellowship and honest sharing. I had never been happier in my life. But then a disturbing event on Sunday morning almost ruined the whole experience for me. The day started out great as we all gathered in the chapel to pray and worship before breakfast. The Holy Spirit filled the room as the chorus of men's voices sang: "God is so good . . . God is so good . . . he's so good to me."

As I entered into singing with the other men, I was shocked to hear a blasphemous thought emerge from somewhere within me: *What in the hell is so good about God?* This thought was quickly followed by a series of rapid-fire questions that I used to interrogate my heart: *Where did that blasphemy come from? Do I really believe that God isn't good? I am the leader, and here I am questioning God's goodness. What is wrong with me? Maybe I should resign on the spot.* As these thoughts raced through my mind, I stood there defenseless. Without an answer, I pushed them out of my mind and proceeded to serve the men on the weekend. I was too ashamed to tell another soul.

I now understand this was a spiritual assault from the "accuser" (Rv 12:10), attempting to steal the joy and graces of the CRHP experience and keep me from all that was still to come. But why did it come from inside me? Why would I question God's goodness? I know God is good; why did I ever doubt it? At the time, I never explored the possibility that my blasphemous thoughts about God were revealing unhealed places buried in my heart for many years. That insight would come later as I continued in the renewal process.

The normal protocol in CRHP is to turn the reigns over to the next team after giving the weekend seminar. But because the new team was short on manpower, we were invited to serve another term with them. This turned out to be an incredible gift from the Father. None of us were ready to let go of this life-changing formation process, and each of us longed to offer this gift to more men.

Following another six-month process of forming community and preparing, it came time to offer the next weekend seminar with our new team. As the weekend approached, something very strange was going on inside me. Unlike previous weekend seminars, where I couldn't wait to go, I wanted to stay home this time. Knowing I had an obligation to the team, I went anyway; but even when I got to our team meeting Friday night, I remained flat and lifeless. That evening I pulled aside one of the men on our team whom I knew from the prayer group in our parish. In speaking with him, I discovered I had to do some spiritual housecleaning, as a result of reading some occult books a few years earlier.

John helped me to see that these books were doorways for spiritual oppression. I acknowledged my sin but didn't make a formal confession until the next evening. After our conversation, I went straight to bed. Words cannot begin to describe the emptiness and hellishness I felt as I tried to go to sleep that night. Surely something inside me was wrong. Having unmasked some hidden evil, I had trouble sleeping that night and woke up the next morning with the same emptiness.

Before breakfast, I greeted the men as best I could, relieved only by seeing my brother Bart show up as a participant for the weekend. This was a huge step for him. Recently cut by the Tampa Bay Buccaneers professional football team, he was looking for purpose in his life. I wanted this to be a life-changing weekend for him, but in my present state of mind it was hard to get too excited. I spent that entire Saturday in the same spiritual desolation. Everyone around me was full of the Holy Spirit, while I sat there empty and lifeless for fourteen long and grueling hours. Around nine o'clock that night, I was worn out and tempted to skip confessions and the closing Mass. But John asked me to read the first reading from the New Testament during the Mass. That meant I would have to stay up, despite my angst. I decided I might as well go to confession since I was waiting. It was a good choice and, though I didn't realize it at the time, a significant turning point.

When Mass started, I noticed I felt less oppressed. When I stood up to read the passage, I felt as though a light switch had suddenly been turned on. I sensed the Holy Spirit's presence, awakening my spirit for the first time in two days. Later during communion, I knew Jesus' Real Presence in the Eucharist as never before. With my joy restored, I was wide awake and now didn't want to go to sleep. I am glad I didn't because a few hours later God changed my life forever. An experience such as this is hard to put into words, but I will try my best to communicate it. Those of you who have had similar experiences will understand. Those of you who haven't, I hope it will increase your hunger and thirst for a personal encounter of your own.

At three o'clock that Sunday morning (long after my normal bed-time), six men from our team felt led to kneel together to pray and offer praise and worship to God. Like the disciples at Pentecost, we devoted ourselves "with one accord to prayer" (Acts 1:14a) and were soon "filled with the holy Spirit" (Acts 2:4a). As the Spirit came upon each one of us (without visible tongues of fire), we began to praise God with a fervor none of us had ever experienced before. Two of my friends were praising Jesus in English with every fiber of their being. Their voices sounded as if they were in heaven praising with the holy angels and all the saints. A few seconds later, the young man to my right began to praise in a foreign language inspired by the Holy Spirit. Though I didn't understand the words, it was the most beautiful prayer I had ever heard, rivaled only by the praise of the men across from me praying in a language I could comprehend.

I was fully enjoying what was happening with my friends when suddenly I felt a rush of energy inside me, like "rivers of living water" gushing from my depths (see Jn 7:38). I felt like I was going to explode with joy, as the love of God was poured into my heart through the Holy Spirit (Rom 5:5). This love felt otherworldly, unlike any love I had ever experienced in my life. I began to laugh and cry almost simultaneously and thought of the scripture passage where Jesus said that new wine could burst an old wineskin (Mk 2:22). My restricted soul felt like that old wineskin about to burst with the explosion of God's love. In that moment, I received the gift of a praise language—in baby talk. God was teaching me to become like a little child to receive his kingdom (Mt 18:1–4). I couldn't believe this was happening to me. I identified with the members of Cornelius's household when Peter preached to them after Pentecost: "The Holy Spirit fell upon all . . . for they could hear them speaking in tongues and glorifying God" (Acts 10:44, 46). I had been praying for the gifts of the Spirit for years and gave up hope three years earlier when nothing seemed to happen during the Life in the Spirit seminar. But now, when I least expected it, I was surprised by these amazing manifestations of the Holy Spirit.

What a dramatic shift. After my anguish of the previous twenty-four hours, I was now heading to bed with the bliss of heaven in my soul. This was the kind of peak experience that I had witnessed in other people, but never thought possible in my life. God amazed me with his goodness and mercy. Little did I realize he was only beginning to pour out his gifts on me and the other men. On only three hours of sleep, I woke up the next morning with the refreshment and joy of a child at Christmas. I cried with joy for most of that day, no small thing since I hadn't cried at all for the entire twenty years since my parents divorced. Jesus was healing me in ways I couldn't even imagine.

That entire Sunday was incredible; three events especially stand out in my memory. The first occurred early Sunday morning as we all sang together in the chapel. Can you guess what we were singing? Yes, the same song from six months earlier when I had the blasphemous thought about God. As we sang "God is so good . . . he's so good to me," I believed every word in the depths of my heart.

A few minutes later, still in the chapel, I received another outpouring of the Holy Spirit as my brother Bart prayed out loud and our pastor Father Mike and my close friend Wyatt silently prayed over me. My good and generous Father couldn't have orchestrated things any better. When I left the chapel and went out into the main hall, I proclaimed boldly and joyously to any who would hear: "I will go anywhere in the world and tell everyone how *good* God is."

Finally, I understood why I had entertained those blasphemous thoughts from six months earlier. They came from a deeply rooted belief that I could never please God, no matter how hard I tried. My theology knew he was good, but my wounded heart believed some lies about him. These lies were hard to articulate but sounded something like this: *God is a cruel taskmaster who always demands more. He is never here for me.* These wounds originated years earlier from my broken relationship with my dad. I loved my dad, and I knew he loved me, but after he left I silently judged him in my heart as a good father who turned bad and could not be trusted. I never voiced those words out loud. They remained hidden in my heart. Out of that wound, I projected all of this unconsciously onto God the Father. Not trusting him, I had been trying to earn his love. I was striving to please him but felt it was never good enough, because I couldn't feel his love. Until this outpouring of grace, I didn't really believe he loved me. Finally I knew his love. With the barriers around my heart removed, I could now receive what he had always desired to give me. And there was more.

Judgement
Others receive love —   *Trust*

The Father continued lavishing his gifts that weekend, not only for me, but also for my brother Bart, for the other men on the weekend seminar, and finally for my wife Margie and our girls when I returned home. The gifts to Bart and the other men came almost simultaneously a few hours after our experience in the chapel that morning. Bart's blessing also blessed me deeply. I had written Bart a letter telling him how much I loved him and how proud I was of him. After reading it he came over to meet me in the middle of the room. When he reached out his hand to thank me, one of the men on our team, Fern, pushed us together and said in his broken English, "Brothers hug." With that, Bart and I embraced each other, immediately breaking into tears as the Holy Spirit ministered to each of our hearts. Bart, who was five years old when Dad left, later told me that the Father spoke to him at that moment: "I am a father to the fatherless. I am your father." Is it any coincidence that the talk before this was on the "Father's Loving Care"? While Bart and

I were embracing, an anointing of the Father's love was released in the room. His presence was so thick that every man who was present broke down in tears, each one experiencing a personal touch of the Father's incredible love. It was truly an amazing event, one that I will never forget.

Before the weekend, I had prayed that I would really know God and be able to love Margie in an entirely new way. Jesus answered these prayers beyond my wildest imagination. I could never have fathomed the events that happened on that weekend, especially with the way the weekend began with me in such utter desolation. Arriving home that evening after the retreat, I was still full of the Holy Spirit, emanating his love and joy. When I saw Margie, I felt a love for her that was brand new, no doubt a manifestation of the love I had just received. My eyes were opened to see my young wife's beauty and goodness in an entirely new way. I wrapped my arms around her and embraced her as never before. Though we had much to work through and still do, it was a new beginning in many ways. After doubting our love for years, we both knew the certainty of our love for each other in that moment. After holding Margie, I couldn't wait to embrace Carrie and Kristen, who were twelve and ten at the time. My heart was full, and I wanted to share it with the ones I loved the most.

My personal transformation and spiritual renewal soon affected many others, including members of my extended family as well as my professional relationships. A process called Family Reconstruction became a major catalyst, where the Holy Spirit led me to face my wounds from when Dad left.[3] On CRHP, my heavenly Father restored my relationship with him. Through the Family Reconstruction, his healing embrace transformed my relationship with my earthly father.

In the years following, most of my family members have also had profound experiences on Christ Renews His Parish retreats and with Family Reconstructions of their own. Some of the most amazing experiences, which I will share later in the book, involved my brother Dave.

One by one, God provided opportunities for each of my family members to experience their own personally fitted graces resulting in their own healing, which inevitably brought about more healing for the rest of the family as well. And it didn't stop there. This wave of healing graces, through the power of the Holy Spirit, spread to the professional community. After attending a Christian Therapist Conference together, several of my colleagues and I founded a Christ-Centered Family Reconstruction community that met once a month for the next twenty years. Thousands of people have received healing and transformation through God's love pouring out of this community.

All I can say is, *God is so good*. Even though I had doubted his goodness, due to my distorted perceptions of him, he still revealed his merciful love to me and healed the wounds that kept my heart bound for years (see 1 Jn 4:8; Ps 103:1–14). His healing love reached my wife, children, extended family, and many others in my parish and professional communities. God does not play favorites (see Heb 10:34–35). He offers the same love for you, your family, and those your life touches. Do you want to know his goodness? If so, follow me through this book, as we come to discover his goodness in the person of Jesus. We begin by encountering Jesus as the Good Teacher in chapter 2.

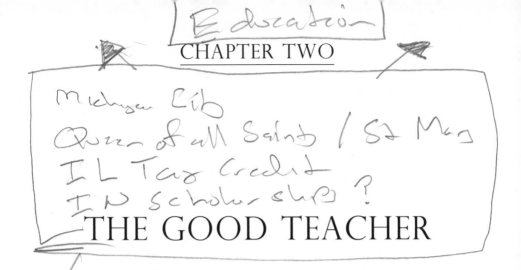

CHAPTER TWO

THE GOOD TEACHER

Modern man listens more willingly to witnesses than to teachers, and if he does listen to teachers, it is because they are witnesses.

Pope Paul VI,
Evangelization in the Modern World

How did you first come to know about Jesus? As children many of us are taught about him through our parents, teachers, and pastors and then come to learn about him ourselves in the gospel stories. These early encounters with Jesus—the Good Teacher (e.g., Lk 18:18; Mt 19:16) serve as our most basic and fundamental experience of God. They also introduce us to his healing love. His teaching brings us into true freedom (Jn 8:31–32).

The greatest poverty in the world is spiritual poverty. When children are not introduced to Jesus early in life, they fill themselves with the garbage of the world. Even children growing up in nominally Christian homes are often starving to know the truth. What a tragedy that even in many Catholic schools today, Jesus and his teaching are not the focal point.

My experience during eleven years of Catholic schooling was quite the opposite. From beginning to end, I was taught "the way and the truth and the life" (Jn 14:6). In most every class, with few exceptions, our teachers taught us solid truth and showed us by their example the way to live in Christ. Most of these teachers (lay people, nuns, coaches, and priests) were faithful witnesses of the Gospel. Far from perfect, they lived what they taught with a certain measure of authenticity and fidelity. I could trust their teaching because they demonstrated it in their lives.

These teachers were building on the foundation that my parents laid for my siblings and me from the time we were born. Until things started falling apart, we were provided solid training in faith. Almost imperceptibly we were being formed as disciples of Jesus, not with a repressive religious atmosphere, but with the ordinary moments of loving interactions and faithful living as a family. Through their teaching, discipline, and mostly by their day-to-day example, my parents taught us to build our house on the rock of Christ, by actively practicing what we were taught (Mt 7:24). Love was the norm in our home, allowing us to implicitly trust our parents and the God they revealed through word and action. I look back with much gratitude for all my parents taught us and sacrificed on our behalf.

As a young boy, I loved both of my parents but naturally looked to my dad as my primary role model. He was my hero. I wanted to become like him in every way possible. Dad was handsome, intelligent, athletic, and the kind of dad who both played and prayed with his children. He got down on our level and played with us for hours, while still maintaining his authority as father and head of household. A firm disciplinarian, he also lost his temper periodically, causing me to feel intimidated at those times. But after yelling, he would inevitably come back and tenderly apologize for hurting my feelings.

In our presence, especially during my first ten years, Dad lived what he taught. Following his example was like breathing the air. We all modeled after him without being aware we were doing it. That is what made it so difficult when my parents started fighting and I discovered Dad was living a duplicitous life. Dave and I unwittingly followed him, both in virtue and in sin. During our early years, we followed Dad's good example on the "road that leads to life" (Mt 7:14), but when Dad starting wandering over to the road to destruction, Dave and I continued blindly walking in the same direction.

We later found out that Dad was smoking, drinking, and crossing boundaries with women, all the while "hiding" it from Mom and us. Dave and I were doing similar things and hiding it from our parents, teachers, and priests. We started smoking, stealing, and looking at Playboy magazines in grade school and eventually began drinking and crossing boundaries with girls in our early teens. We were blindly following Dad's footsteps, just as Jesus had warned: "Can a blind person guide a blind person? Will not both fall into a pit? . . . When fully trained, every disciple will be like his teacher" (Lk 6:39–40).

The worst part is that we all knew better. With our foundations solidly formed in Jesus' teaching, we understood we were wrong every time we violated God's commandments. No matter how much we rationalized our behavior, we still had no excuse. Otherwise we wouldn't have kept our sins hidden. God wasn't fooled; we were only making fools of ourselves with our self-deception (Jas 1:22; 1 Pt 1:13). Eventually each one of us would have to reap the consequences of our destructive behaviors, just as the scriptures warned: "Make no mistake: God is not mocked, for a person will reap only what he sows" (Gal 6:7).

Dad and Dave suffered the most, because they turned their backs on Jesus for a long time. They paid the price for many years. Somehow, by the grace of God, I was preserved from following completely in their footsteps. With the help of my mom, good teachers, coaches, and priests, I turned back to Jesus and his teaching in tenth grade (though far from perfectly). My Catholic education was a big part of my healing process. It provided the foundation that would keep me protected, and headed on the right path, until I encountered the Father's love many years later.

A critical turning point for me came during ninth grade, a year after Dad left. I was lost and in need of direction. I sat in the back row of Mr. Rentz's math class at North Miami Junior High, dazed and disoriented from all that had taken place the previous year. I hardly recognized myself in this strange new environment, which seemed more like a three-ring circus than a school. To make matters worse, there were few ringleaders. Students outwardly disrespected teachers, and teachers passively put up with it.

The fact that I was transitioning into a new school didn't help make my adjustment any easier. I was the outsider, the northern kid with no tan and few friends. I had fallen so far behind in my schoolwork that I gave up caring about my grades and resigned myself to another D in math.

Apparently, my teacher, Mr. Rentz, had other ideas. He taught with great enthusiasm and wanted all his students to love math as much as he did. His passion, coupled with his firm, caring approach, commanded respect from his students. His class was completely different from most of the others. For some reason his opinion mattered to me, and I didn't want to disappoint him. Even more, I didn't want to be embarrassed in front of the class. To avoid being called on, I hid in the last row, hoping he wouldn't notice my presence.

My strategy worked for a while, but inevitably, Mr. Rentz called on me to come to the front chalkboard to solve a math problem. Reluctantly, I made my way to the front of the class, unsure how I was going to bluff my way through the problem. Having fallen so far behind, I couldn't even fake an answer. As I was preparing myself to be humiliated in front of everyone, Mr. Rentz surprised me. Instead of shaming me in the presence of my classmates, he encouraged me, coaching me through the problem, and offering to help me catch up after class was over. After school, when I met with him, he continued encouraging me, telling me he knew I was capable of doing the work.

Mr. Rentz's actions communicated that he believed in me and cared about me. That night, I went home and worked on math problems for hours. This pattern continued for many weeks until I eventually caught up with the class. By the end of the school year, I had earned an A in math. Mr. Rentz was proud of me, and I was pretty pleased with myself. It was a new beginning. This renewed confidence, good grades, and passion for learning continued through high school, into college, and all the way through graduate school. To this day, I love to study, learn, and teach.

I don't recall if I ever thanked Mr. Rentz, but I have thanked God for him. Mr. Rentz revealed the face of Jesus to this lost teenager. For me, he was the embodiment of the Good Teacher at a time when I didn't know how to encounter Jesus directly. Isn't it amazing how one caring act from a teacher can radically impact a student's life? Rather than follow the path of my older brother Dave, who dropped out of school in tenth grade, my life took an entirely different trajectory. Because he cared about me, I cared about myself again.

TAKE A MOMENT

Take a moment to consider which teachers in your life most represented Jesus to you.

- Did any teachers help you get back on track in your life? Who and how? *So Many   7th grade   HS Math   College Lit*

- Which teachers helped awaken your passions, interests, and God's calling in your life? *Mush   Father*

- Which teachers were good role models, by living what they taught? *— High school mush   Father O'Donnell   — College literature*

I now see my Christian education as a precious gift from God, but I took it largely for granted, until I didn't have it anymore. Going to college was a real eye opener. Except for my ninth grade year, my entire education up to that point took place in Catholic schools.

Only after leaving did I realize how good my education in grade school and high school had been. Some courses at Columbia continued to build on that good foundation from high school. By studying St. Augustine and the philosophers of Western culture, we saw how art, philosophy, law, and classical music beautifully expressed the truth of the Gospel throughout the centuries. I could see clearly how all of Western civilization had been built on the foundation of Jesus Christ and the teachings of the Church, at least up until the Enlightenment period of the seventeenth and eighteenth centuries.

I saw some of the bad fruit of the so-called Enlightenment in other classes and teachers, who seemed to magnify the cultural lies more than expound on the truth of the Gospel. A perfect example was my first elective: "Introduction to Philosophy." Anticipating a stimulating topic, I hurried to class and quickly realized the man with the long stringy hair standing up front was my professor. He reminded me some of my brother Dave, who by then had long hair and was heavily into drugs. Even my professor's philosophy of life sounded like Dave's. What I heard went something like this: "If you are looking for some meaning in life, give it up man. There isn't any. There's just experience; some of it good, and some not so good."

I was stunned to hear these words coming out of a professor's mouth. This was quite a contrast from the priests and religious brothers and sisters who taught me in Catholic schools, where everything had meaning and purpose. Before I could recover from the initial shock, my professor continued: "I woke up this morning and took some 'uppers' (amphetamines) to get high, at lunch I smoked some dope (marijuana) to keep me mellow, and I'll smoke another joint after dinner. When I go to bed tonight, I will pop some 'downers' (depressants) to help me sleep."

The word philosophy means "love of wisdom." How could I trust this guy to teach me anything about wisdom in life? Mind you, I was not fully and authentically living the truth myself; I had no right to throw any stones of condemnation in his direction (see Jn 8:7). But that didn't prevent me from copping a superior attitude, which began years earlier when I had formed judgments against my dad and brother.

My life had meaning and purpose, something his didn't seem to have, but he was at least upfront. He lived what he claimed to believe and was honest about sharing it. On my end, I was picking and choosing the aspects of my faith I wanted to practice, all the while rationalizing and hiding my sins behind a mask of self-righteousness. I was playing the hypocrite, but Jesus saw right through my facade:

> Why do you notice the splinter in your brother's eye, but do not perceive the wooden beam in your own? How can you say to your brother, "Brother, let me remove that splinter in your eye," when you do not even notice the wooden beam in your own eye? You hypocrite! Remove the wooden beam from your eye first; then you will see clearly to remove the splinter in your brother's eye. (Lk 6:41–42)

I judged my brother and anyone who resembled him, yet I remained just as much in need of a savior as they did. I now think back to that philosophy teacher with compassion and wonder what he was running away from in his life. He too needed a good teacher to build his confidence and teach him the truth, offering him hope. I can only wonder who broke his trust at some point in life. There had to be something that would have caused him to completely give up hope the way Dad and Dave had done.

Though I judged this teacher under the pretext of Christian values, I was acting more like the self-righteous Pharisees than Jesus. There is nothing Christ-like about judging another from an attitude of superiority. Jesus did not judge or condemn in this way. Though his judgment is just, he didn't come into this world to judge us. Rather, he came to reveal the Father's mercy and compassion (Jn 3:17–21). His mercy triumphs over judgment (see Jas 2:13).

I knew the scripture about God's mercy overcoming judgment, but it would take many years for this truth to penetrate my heart. The catalyst for this deeper conversion came from a very unlikely source: the movie *Good Will Hunting*. It started out inauspiciously, when my wife and I decided to go to a movie and dinner for our weekly date night. Margie chose the movie. I didn't stop to check to see that it was R rated. But as soon as I started watching it, the language and an implied sex scene troubled me. I was ready to leave, but Margie seemed engrossed in the movie, which offended me even more. Silently, I sat there judging her for enjoying the movie. Let's just say, my state of mind was not conducive to a romantic evening together.

As the movie progressed, I began to relax and found myself engaged in the story, which turned out to be surprisingly redemptive. Will Hunting, the main character, was a badly abused but brilliant young man. His wounds kept him from living up to his full potential. He ran from himself and was totally out of touch with his own heart. Sound like anyone else you know? Will's therapist, Sean McGuire, had been himself horribly abused as a child and could see right through Will's facade.

In the most gripping scene of the movie, Sean relentlessly pursues Will's wounded heart, eventually breaking through Will's defenses. As this scene unfolds, I suddenly realized I was watching a modern-day version of the prodigal son story.[1] As Will (the prodigal son) is sobbing in the arms of his therapist (an image of the Father), he is finally able to release the torrents of pain and disappointment he has been carrying his entire life.

Sean, the therapist, also reveals the powerful love of Jesus. Like Jesus, Sean knew Will's suffering intimately from his own experience, which enabled him to identify with Will's brokenness. Watching all this unfold, I finally understood the meaning of the title of the movie. It is a clever play on words: behind all his sin, wounds, and defenses, Will deeply desired what is good, and had been hunting for goodwill all his life. Abused and overlooked as a child, he finally found someone in Sean who understood him and revealed God's love to him.

As I was making this connection with the prodigal son story (Lk 16), I began wondering who represented the self-righteous older brother. I was shocked to realize it was me. I had been standing back judging my own brother most of my life, along with my dad, and now with my wife. Anyone close to me that didn't measure up to my standards of morality was a possible target of my self-righteous judgments.

Suddenly, I realized I needed the Father's mercy just as much as they did. Up till then Will's character had been alien to me, but now I could identify with him. I was no better than Will. I too had a huge father wound and was continuing to run from the Father. Like Will, I denied my longing for the Father's embrace and kept myself protected by layers of insulation that surrounded my heart. No matter how hard I tried, like Will, I couldn't fix myself by my intelligence or achievements. I needed Jesus, who knew the depths of my pain and was willing to persist as long as it took to break through these internal barriers. I wanted to be set free and to quit hiding behind the facade of my judgments and pride. I wanted to be found, to be known, and most of all to be embraced.

How ironic and how like God that he would use this R-rated movie that I didn't want to see to expose my superior attitude and reveal the deeper longings of my heart. As I sat there watching the rest of the movie, I felt naked to the core of my being, tears streaming down my face. I was lost in my own world of thought.

I don't even know what happened through the rest of the movie, but I do remember Margie and I heading to the car after it was over. We were holding hands, in silence. Margie is at her very best in moments like these, when she senses genuine vulnerability in me. She waited a few minutes and simply said, "We don't need to go to dinner; let's go home." Then quietly waiting again, she let me talk when I was ready. She was a better therapist in that moment than I had ever been, despite all my years of training and experience.

With tears flowing again, I was only able to get out a few words. "I'm a fraud," I said solemnly. Margie's shocked look let me know that I was doing a poor job of conveying what was going on inside me. I continued telling her about my earlier attitude of superiority and judgment while watching the movie. I proceeded to tell her how I was blown away and convicted by the scene between Will and the therapist. I tried to explain the best I could why I felt like a hypocrite. While spending my entire career teaching people about God's love and healing, I was failing miserably to be an authentic witness of these truths. I was more comfortable hiding behind my knowledge, too afraid to love with Jesus' reckless abandon. I encouraged everyone else to face their brokenness, but I remained resistant to facing my own.

As I continued to pour my heart out, I confessed to Margie all the ways I fell short of being an authentic teacher and therapist, and even more so as her husband. I went on to tell her how much I longed to be a better husband and therapist. I desired to have the boldness to love the way Sean did in the movie but was too afraid to risk opening myself like that. I was trained to keep my professional distance, but deeper than that was the "training" I received through people breaking my trust. I also expressed my desire for the healing that Will received; how I longed to experience a deeper embrace of the Father that would touch the core of my pain.

Margie, not one to analyze much, responded compassionately, "I always felt like there was more hurt there with your dad leaving. I wonder what it will take to completely heal you." I was stunned by her response, both at her incredible insight into my heart that so often felt overlooked, but even more so by her awareness that so much of my pain and falsehood was rooted in my running from my wounds from childhood.

Take a moment to reflect on the judgments you have held towards members of your family or others. *I understood his pain*

NO

- Who did you judge? How did they hurt you?

- Can you identify the specific judgments you held towards them?

- How and when did Jesus open your eyes to the truth?

2000 - I sat on bed looked at Susan This can't go on - I'm so angry I let the anger go & replaced it with love

Similar to Will, I spent most of my twenties searching for truth, while at the same time running from it. I studied world religions, trying to find the common denominator between all of them. I read the Bible as well as other spiritual and self-help books. I attended Catholic Mass and visited churches from many different denominations. I enjoyed learning about the differences in faiths but was afraid to commit my heart to anything or anyone. At the end of it all, though I gained much knowledge, I ended up more confused than when I began. I struggled to understand how the many differences in beliefs could be reconciled. Many were quoting from the same Bible but with exact opposite interpretations. Who and what could I trust to be the truth?

During this time of searching, I kept things mostly at a safe, intellectual level, not venturing too far into my heart, where I felt lost and insecure. I didn't fully trust any authority. I wondered if there was any solid ground to stand on. Maybe the secular atheists were right; is there any such thing as absolute truth? Have you ever asked those questions in your life? If so, you understand how unsettling it can be to question the very foundations of your security. I am sure all these factors contributed to my panic attack in my late twenties.

In the midst of it all, I shared my struggle with some dear friends, Jim and Lois. Jim, thirty years older, would later become one of my

CRHP brothers. I had been friends with him and Lois several years before CRHP. I trusted them both and knew I could go to them to discuss my personal concerns. Moreover, I respected their authentic witness of love and faithfulness, and I trusted them as much as anyone in my life. They lived their faith genuinely, with love and joy.

As I shared my confusion and anxiety, they were both sympathetic and helped me see clearly in the midst of my confusion. Though this particular conversation took place over thirty years ago, I still remember it vividly today. Lois shared a similar confusion from a time earlier in her life. Someone she trusted and admired recommended that she narrow her focus solely to the person of Jesus. When she did, everything became crystal clear, eventually leading her to fall deeply and passionately in love with Jesus. Years later she found the authority of the Catholic Church to be a trustworthy guardian of the Gospel and entered the Church as a convert.

As soon as Lois shared her experience, I knew in my spirit that her wisdom came straight from the Holy Spirit. It is among the best advice I have ever received.

After my conversation with Jim and Lois, I began to search the scriptures with a renewed focus—trying to learn everything I could about Jesus. As a teacher myself, I was first drawn to him as Teacher. It didn't take long to discover that Jesus was more amazing than any teacher I had ever met and unlike all the highly educated teachers of his day. Time and again people were astonished at his teaching. He spoke with authority and "not as the scribes" (Mk 1:22).

The scribes and Pharisees were the learned of Jesus' time, but despite their knowledge, their teaching lacked authority (Mt 23). Though they taught about God, they didn't know him. Jesus said their worship of God was more lip service than real. Their hearts were far from him (Mt 15:8). Everyone they taught could see plainly their lack of authenticity, even if they themselves couldn't.

Jesus was completely different. He spoke out of the essence of his intimacy with the Father. Every word that came out of Jesus' mouth was infused with the power of the Holy Spirit. Unlike any other teacher in the history of the world, Jesus fully lived what he taught and proclaimed exactly what he lived. He provided the fully authentic witness I had been searching for all my life. He was the only one who could fully bear the weight of my admiration, the one person to whom I could entrust my heart.

Jesus oozed humility and his teaching was filled with integrity. When he taught about God's kingdom, he backed it up by demonstrating God's love and power through healing and miracles. He didn't just teach precepts for people to follow, like the other religious leaders; rather, he reached out to people and cared about their deepest needs. Unlike myself and others I knew, Jesus never did anything out of ego or pride but always acted out of love for his Father. His heart overflowed with compassion and mercy for the poor and all who were oppressed in body, mind, or spirit.

The more I studied about this Good Teacher, the more my heart was drawn to him. For the first time since Dad left, I began to fully trust the words of someone in authority. Gradually, my heart began to rest again. I thought to myself, *This is one person who will never let me down.* From that point on, it became easy for me to trust the authority of scripture and eventually the teaching authority of the Church. All of it revealed Jesus, and I knew with confidence that his teaching was fully trustworthy.

Coming to know Jesus in this way was life-changing and deeply healing. For the first time since childhood, I began to feel secure again. But soon, my newfound trust gave way to more fear and anxiety, as I

Jesus didn't have casual students; he had disciples who gave up everything to follow him.

realized I could not remain neutral with Jesus. Jesus didn't have casual students; he had disciples who gave up everything to follow him. They believed in him with their entire lives and followed him everywhere he went. They didn't just sit in school and study to acquire knowledge. They followed Jesus and did everything he did.

I began to comprehend that believing in Jesus was much more than reciting the creed, keeping the commandments, or going to church on Sunday. It required a radical commitment of my life and everything associated with it. Jesus' dialogue with the rich official in Luke's gospel made this abundantly clear.

> Rich Official: Good teacher, what must I do to inherit eternal life?
>
> Jesus: Why do you call me good? No one is good but God alone. You know the commandments, "You shall not commit adultery . . . kill . . . steal . . . bear false witness; honor your father and your mother.
>
> Rich Official: All of these I have observed from my youth.
>
> Jesus: There is still one thing left for you: sell all that you have . . . Come, follow me. (Lk 18:18–22)

Jesus saw this man's genuine goodness and admired him. But he wanted to take away any grounds for this man's self-righteousness or self-reliance, showing that God is the source and origin of all true goodness and that genuine faith requires a radical dependence on God and not on one's self. Jesus is the only good teacher because he is God; he alone is truly good. Otherwise he would have no authority to call this man or any of us to such radical discipleship.

Following Jesus sounds attractive, until we have to give up our self-sufficiency. Aren't we all terrified at some level when we read this story? We try to rationalize it away: does Jesus really require us to let go of everything in order to follow him? Can you relate, or am I the only one who finds this frightening? I am consoled that Pope Francis understands my fear: When teaching on the Beatitudes, he said, "We are afraid of salvation. We need it, but we are afraid. We have to give everything. He is in charge! And we are afraid of this . . . we want control of ourselves."[2]

Remember my encounter with Jesus (in chapter 1), where he challenged me to be "either cold or hot"? I was threatened to the core of my being. I didn't (and to some degree still don't) want to let go of my false securities. I want to live life on my own terms. But that is not life; it is death. Jesus made this perfectly clear: "Whoever seeks to preserve his life will lose it, but whoever loses it [for my sake] will save it" (Lk 17:33).

TAKE A MOMENT

Take a moment to consider how you have been trying to save yourself.

- What self-reliant strategies have you used to try to find fulfillment in life? Go it alone

- Have you given your life completely to Jesus? No

- Do you believe he is fully worthy of your trust? Yes

If you don't fully trust Jesus, don't lie to yourself. Simply be honest with yourself and with him about it. He is The Compassionate Healer, and he invites each one of us to bring our brokenness to him so that he can heal us.

CHAPTER THREE

THE COMPASSIONATE HEALER

Miracles happen. But they need prayer! A courageous prayer, that struggles for that miracle. Not like those prayers of courtesy: Ah, I will pray for you!

Pope Francis,
L'Osservatore Romano

Stepping into the gospel story of Matthew 9:27, imagine that you and I are the two blind people who seek an encounter with Jesus. Until now, we have preferred to stay on the fringes of town rather than face public scrutiny. We are ashamed of our infirmities.

But as stories of miraculous healings circulate throughout our village, we notice an air of excitement among our kinsmen, giving us an unusual sense of hope and boldness. No one has ever seen or heard such things before in our day. Is it possible the long-awaited Messiah has come?

You and I whisper to each other, "Maybe he will heal *us*." It seems impossible, but news of a paralyzed man being cured in the next village buoys our hopes even more. Our sense of anticipation rises, as reports that the healer is heading our way spreads through our village. All around us we hear the buzzing of the crowd. They say he is somewhere on the road in front of us. We stumble along behind the multitude, shouting, "Son of David, have pity on us."

Without warning, the crowd stops abruptly in front of someone's house. The healer has disappeared. Is he inside? Have we missed our chance? Undeterred, we cry out again, with even greater fervor, "Son of David, have pity on us!"

Confident that he hears us, we instinctively quiet ourselves, waiting, hoping that he does not pass us by. For once we *want* to be noticed.

A voice responds from inside the house; the Healer has acknowledged our plea and is coming out to meet us. Within seconds, we feel his presence standing directly in front of us. We hold our breath, as he gently reaches out his hand to touch our eyes; his few words bear an unmistakable authority, and the kindness in his voice pierces our hearts in a way we've never experienced. We feel loved and known by this man, who seconds ago was just a stranger.

As he touches our eyes, we feel power flowing from his hands and warmth spreading out throughout our body. Our eyes flutter and begin to tingle. Suddenly, light flashes in front of us, like the lightning bolts that light up the sky in the middle of a summer storm. Bursts of joyful laughter explode like thunder from our mouths. Within seconds, tears of gratitude pour down our cheeks like torrents of rain. When the clearing comes, we can *see*. Faces all around us are astonished, mirroring our own amazement. Who is this man, and who besides the mighty Elijah has ever restored the sight of ones born blind?

Shocked, we try to make sense of what is happening. Our eyes are drawn to meet the gaze of the Healer. He sees *us*. For some unknown reason, we matter to this man. He treats us with a reverence we have never known before; it is almost too much to bear. Without words, his gentle eyes communicate a desire to heal our entire being.

Our physical healing, astonishing as it is, pales in comparison to the healing he now offers us. Without words, he speaks to the depths of our hearts. His penetrating gaze says it all, offering to restore those areas of our souls that have been blinded by pride, fear, and unbelief. This is too much. Politely, we refuse his offer, averting our eyes to avoid his. We thank him for this incredible treasure of our sight and insist that what he has given us is more generous than we could ever repay.

The Healer smiles with understanding. Perceiving the true motive at work in our hearts, he accepts our protest and sees that underneath our polite exterior, terror lurks like a wounded guard dog, ready to pounce at any moment. For the first time, we wonder if it was a mistake to ask him to heal us. Before our sight was restored we could hide in the false security of the only thing we knew. We had found comfort in the darkness. Seeing and being seen is more terrifying than we imagined. He assures us that he has no intention of violating our will. His motive is pure love, without any strings attached. We have total freedom to choose. His offer to heal remains an open invitation. Reassured, our hearts stop racing. Our bodies relax. But we don't understand. Why were we so afraid? This compassionate healer has only desired good things for us and loved us with love we have never known.

Now let's step outside the gospel story to reflect on our experience. Was that real? "No, of course not," you say. "It was all in our imagination." Yes, at one level that is true, but was it unreal? Is it possible that the imaginative experience we just shared together was real in ways we can't fully comprehend? Leanne Payne, a woman with much experience engaging the faculty of imagination to facilitate deep healing, writes, "The truly imaginative experience is . . . an intuition of the real. It is an acknowledgment of objective realities . . . in their essence . . . it is the experience of receiving from God."[1]

Payne's perspective is shared by many saints and spiritual directors down through the ages, including St. Ignatius of Loyola and St. Frances de Sales. They teach us to stretch our faith by placing ourselves subjectively in the gospel stories. In doing so, we allow ourselves to be transformed by Jesus as we encounter him in faith. Jesus is not limited by time and space. He continues to walk our streets, enter our homes, and restore our hearts. He wants to heal us. Are we willing?

As you entered into the story in Matthew's gospel, did you allow yourself to feel what it is like to be afflicted with physical and spiritual infirmities? Could you identify with the hopelessness that comes from living with a condition for so long that you doubt you will ever be healed? Do you know what it feels like to be overlooked and feel isolated? Each of those experiences has been familiar to me at some point in my life and I would think for you as well.

On the other hand, do you also know what it feels like to be healed by Jesus; pierced to your depths by his gaze; deeply touched by his kindness; comforted by his authority; and relieved of your longstanding affliction by his powerful anointing? As I shared in chapter 1, I have experienced his healing presence in these ways. His joy was like an explosion in me. I didn't know whether to laugh or cry. My heart raced with fear, wondering whether I would lose control if I allowed Jesus to heal the deeper places of my heart. Can you relate to any of these experiences? I've never been physically blind, so I don't know what it feels like to be healed in this way. But I have witnessed miracles of healing with people who were physically blind.[2] It is truly amazing. I also know what it is like to be confronted by Jesus in my spiritual blindness. When Jesus spoke to me at the prayer breakfast telling me to be "cold or hot", he went on to show me my spiritual blindness and poverty in the same passage:

> For you say, "I am rich and affluent and have no need of anything," and yet do not realize that you are wretched, pitiable, poor, blind, and naked. I advise you to buy from me gold refined by fire so that you may be rich, and white garments to put on so that your shameful nakedness may not be exposed, and buy ointment to smear on your eyes so that you may see. Those whom I love, I reprove and chastise. Be earnest, therefore, and repent. (Rv 3:17–19)

Notice the phrase "Those whom I love, I reprove and chastise." At the time, Jesus' words didn't feel like love. I felt threatened, not comforted. Anxiety overwhelmed me; I was not ready to let down my walls of self-protection. But Jesus' words snuck in behind my normally formidable defenses. Looking back I recognize that Jesus was saying these things to me out of love. I am now eternally grateful for his strong rebuke. I was living in a kind of darkness, blinded from seeing my hidden infirmities and sins. Jesus' words were like the surgeon's knife, removing the deadly cancer of pride out of my soul. Throughout my late teens and early twenties I really believed I was fine; I didn't need anything from anyone, not even my Savior. I rationalized my many sins and denied my badly wounded heart, broken into pieces by my parents' divorce. I was spiritually and psychologically ill; although in desperate need of healing, I had only the faintest awareness of these needs, until Jesus pierced my facade. I was like the Pharisees who had an intellectual knowledge of God but denied his power to heal.

TAKE A MOMENT

Take a moment to consider how you have denied your need for healing.

- Have you ever hidden behind a religious facade in your own life? *No* What were you hiding behind the facade?

- Can you think of a time when Jesus exposed your facade and you felt threatened? What happened as a result?

When most people in the gospels experience Jesus' healing miracles they are astonished. Jesus, in contrast, is not astonished by the miracles, but by the people who claim to believe in God but deny his powerful love manifested right before their eyes (Mk 6:6). Which ones are we more like? Are we amazed when we see Jesus' powerful love demonstrated? Or do we read or listen to the gospel accounts with a certain familiarity and indifference? Do we believe Jesus wants to heal today? Or do we avoid genuine encounters with Jesus, hiding instead behind religious pride or intellectual arrogance, which is merely a mask covering our hopelessness and unbelief?

Most of us still believe in healing, as long as it is the slow and methodical kind, through doctors, medications, and therapeutic practices. That is all good, but do we leave room for Jesus? Do you know one of the words used to describe Jesus' healing in the gospels is *therapeua*, which is where we get our word for therapist? Jesus is the best therapist and physician anyone could ever have. But we regularly deny that he is physician of our souls and bodies. Is there any place in our life for healing that is not based on science and medical training?

Please don't misunderstand me. Solid training and good science are gifts from God, when fully integrated with our faith.[3] As a therapist I have been through years of training; and I remain grateful that my doctors have received considerable training as well. I agree with Francis MacNutt when he says, "In no way do I conceive prayer for healing as denying the need for doctors, nurses, counselors, psychiatrists, or pharmacists. God works in all those ways to heal the sick."[4] My point is that we have come to treat modern medicine and psychology as gods while denying the true physician of our souls and bodies. This needs to change!

Our faith needs to be stretched so we can openly receive the healing that Jesus freely desires to give to us.

If healing is essential to Christianity, as Pope Benedict XVI asserts, it needs to be restored to its rightful place in the Church and in all of our lives. Our faith needs to be stretched so we can openly receive the healing that Jesus freely desires to give to us. Are we willing to have our capacity to receive from God expanded?

A significant time of faith stretching for me came a number of years ago when a pastor friend of mine invited me to go on a healing mission to Brazil with him. Gary, who now has a worldwide healing ministry, is the author of *Open My Eyes, Lord*.[5] When I met him, he was the pastor of a local church and taught at the school of ministry where I taught. I knew him to be an honest and sober man. After returning from Brazil the first time, he recounted story after story of miraculous healings: deaf people received the gift of hearing; blind people had their sight restored; dumb people suddenly were able to speak; physically disabled men and women jumped up and walked; and people without hope were filled with hope. If I hadn't known him so well, I wouldn't have believed what he was telling me.

But Gary's excitement was infectious. My spirit rejoiced as I heard his testimonies. The stories sounded as if they were straight out of the gospels. And by the grace of God, I immediately knew it was all true. But believing his stories didn't require a huge stretch of faith on my part. That wouldn't occur until I accepted Gary's invitation to accompany him on his next mission trip to Brazil.

I have come to realize that our faith becomes real only when it is put to the test courageously. As Pope Francis said, "A prayer that calls for an extraordinary action must be a prayer that involves all of us, as though our very life depends on it. In prayer, you have to put yourself to the test."[6] One of my favorite illustrations of this point is the story of a tightrope walker who went across Niagara Falls pushing a wheelbarrow. After he walked over it the first time, he asked the crowd how many believed he could do it again. Nearly everyone raised his or her hand. Impressed with their faith, he pointed to a young man in front and said, "Okay, get in the wheelbarrow, and I will push you across."

I was like that guy that "got in" after Gary's third trip. He had been telling me all about the miracles he witnessed after the first two trips. After his third trip, he invited me into the wheelbarrow. I knew that it wasn't Gary but Jesus who was inviting me to step out in faith. My spiritual director confirmed I was called to go. Six months later, I found myself in Londrina, Brazil, serving on a team of seventy Christians from all over the world, representing Christ's body from the nations. Our team physically represented Jesus, the life-giving physician of souls and bodies, to the hurting people of Londrina.[7]

During my first two days in Brazil, I had opportunities to pray with people who needed inner healing, something I had been doing for years. Out of the hundreds of people there who needed prayer, I was led to pray for two women who had been sexually abused as children. In desperation and hopelessness, they had each attempted suicide during the past year. My heart was stirred with compassion for them, and I desired to do all I could to help relieve them of their intense suffering. But I was troubled by the severe time limitations.

Believing Jesus would heal these women of their wounds from sexual abuse was not much of a stretch of faith for me. I had witnessed many such healings before. The real stretching was that we had so little time to minister to each woman. The time we had was further slowed by the necessity of an interpreter. My normal experience back home was that sexual abuse wounds often took months or even years to heal. Here, in Brazil, we didn't have months, or even hours. It seemed ridiculous to me that we had less than thirty minutes to pray with each woman. I was still thinking as a therapist. I wondered to myself if it was even ethical to start praying with them, given the limited time and with no opportunity to follow up.

But in prayer, our small team of men and women sensed the Holy Spirit give us the go-ahead to proceed. I surrendered my doubts and concerns and then sat in awe as Jesus healed and comforted these precious daughters of his. What ordinarily takes months and years was happening right before my eyes in minutes. This healing miracle occurred twice in the same day, as if Jesus seemed to emphasize that he really was capable of doing this more than once.

Giving us the gift of supernatural wisdom to discern the roots of the problem, the Holy Spirit moved through us as skilled surgeons, cutting out the cancerous memories. Jesus quickly restored the core identity of these women as beloved daughters of the Father. Miraculously, they were freed from suicidal despair and brought to experience a hope they had never known. While praying, they felt a release of the trauma they had been carrying their entire life, as well as the shame that had kept them crippled since childhood.

As you might imagine we were all incredulous with joy and filled with heartfelt gratitude toward God. These once-depressed suicidal women now radiated a beauty and joyfulness that still lingers in my mind. The next day, both women came up to greet us along with their husbands; they were beaming. With shared delight we joined hands and together thanked Jesus for the miraculous gift he had given to each one of us. My few words of Portuguese were inadequate to express the depth of gratitude I felt toward our Compassionate Healer. Thankfully, their radiant faces revealed the glory of God and said everything that needed to be spoken.

After two days of similar experiences, my heart was full. I could have returned home happily, but I sensed there was more to learn and that the people were in great need of further healing. As I prayed, I felt the Holy Spirit nudging me to accept another faith challenge. That evening, a young Chinese woman from our team sat on the bus next to me.

We spoke about the challenge of ministering to the deepest needs in people's lives. Every time we stepped out in faith to pray we were taking a huge risk, not only for ourselves but especially for those with whom we were praying. Since there are no guarantees that our prayers will be answered in the way we desire, we do not want to do more harm than good. What benefit is it if we build up their hopes and then leave them disappointed? I shared my lack of faith in praying for certain miracles of physical healing. She understood completely and shared her testimony from earlier that day.

Recognizing her own lack of faith and fearfulness, she spoke this simple prayer to Jesus: "You know I can't heal anyone. You alone have the power to heal. I acknowledge my dependence on you. I will pray for anyone you ask me to pray for and leave the results to you." Her eyes lit up in amazement as she shared the events that transpired hours after her prayer. She had opportunities to pray for several people who needed miracles of physical healing. Everyone she prayed for was healed that day. It seemed too good to be true, but I was reminded of Matthew's gospel where Jesus healed the multitudes:

> Jesus went around to all the towns and villages, teaching in their synagogues, proclaiming the gospel of the kingdom, and curing every disease and illness. At the sight of the crowds, his heart was moved with pity for them because they were troubled and abandoned, like sheep without a shepherd. (Mt 9:35–36)

Jesus felt compassion for all of the people and cured every disease and illness. If that was true in Galilee, was it possible that he still desired to do the same thing here in Londrina, Brazil? Amazed by this woman's story, I felt inspired to follow her example of faith. So with some trepidation, but learning from my Chinese sister in Christ, I abandoned myself to Jesus and imitated her simple prayer: "Jesus, I believe you brought me here to teach me, to stretch my faith, and to allow me to minister to your precious children. Lead me. I know you are the Healer. Apart from you, I can do nothing (Jn 15:5). I submit myself entirely to you; may your will be done."

The next day I was immediately tested in what I had prayed the night before, as I had opportunities to pray with four different people that day. One was legally blind. Another couldn't walk. Two others had problems with their shoulders. In all four cases, the afflictions were readily apparent, ones that, if healed, could be verified immediately. But we would also know immediately if nothing happened. Remembering my prayer, I stepped out in faith, trusting in Jesus' life-giving presence and not in my own ability to heal anybody. It was a moment of extreme spiritual poverty and blind faith. One by one, the interpreter and I prayed for each person. Amazingly, all four were completely healed. Again, I was touched by the knowledge of the Lord's nearness and loving-kindness and compassion for his lost and wounded sheep.

During the rest of my eight days in Brazil, I witnessed many other miracles. It became so "normal" that I understood what Francis MacNutt meant after praying for people around the world: "The results of prayer have been extraordinary—so much so that what once would have astonished me, I now take for granted. The extraordinary has become ordinary. And that is the way I think the healing ministry should be: an ordinary, normal part of the Christian life."[8]

TAKE A MOMENT

- Can you remember an experience when the extraordinary became ordinary? How did you respond?

- Think of a time when you stepped out in faith and trusted Jesus. How did he confirm your faith? What happened?

I wondered what it would be like when I returned home, where it didn't seem normal at all. My first Sunday back at our parish, the Father had a special treat waiting for me. The gospel reading from Matthew confirmed all that I had experienced in Brazil. In it, John the Baptist, who was in prison, sent a messenger to Jesus asking, "Are you the one?" Jesus responds by quoting the Messianic prophecy from Isaiah: "Go and tell John what you have seen and heard: the blind regain their sight, the lame walk . . . the deaf hear" (Lk 7:20, 22). I had heard that gospel passage dozens of times in the past. But for the first time it really registered. Tingling energy went down my spine. I knew beyond a shadow of any doubt that God was validating my experience in Brazil. These were the very things I saw and heard: the blind seeing, the deaf hearing, and the lame walking.

The same Compassionate Healer still desires to bring all his children to wholeness. I sat in awe, realizing he chose me to share in this life-changing ministry. Suddenly, it dawned on me: this experience was not just for Brazil. The Father was asking me to bring what I learned back to the United States. I realized I needed to ask our pastor to begin a monthly healing service at our parish. Father Mike not only agreed to support it but also has been there faithfully serving ever since. Our parish is called Good Shepherd Catholic Church, and to me and for many of his parishioners, Father Mike beautifully represents the Good Shepherd's compassionate love, always reaching out to his lost and wounded sheep.

Our monthly healing services are still occurring ten years later. They remain quite simple, usually with a small team of ministers lovingly serving any who come for prayer. The Compassionate Healer is present every time. You can imagine our joy when a young boy with severe eye problems was healed at our second meeting. Many others have received healings of various infirmities, ranging from cancer to depression. Not everyone has received instant and miraculous healing, but all have been touched by Jesus' compassionate heart in some particular way.

One of the most challenging and heartrending situations involved a young man who became quadriplegic after a tragic car accident. He was the driver and one of his closest friends was killed. As you might imagine, this young man's spirit became paralyzed by the crushing shame and guilt he carried every day since the accident. A group of us, including his aunt, a woman of strong faith, prayed for him and his mother that night. We saw only slight improvement in his body, as one of his hands regained some nerve sensation. It was enough, however, to build his faith and let him know that Jesus was truly present and working. That became the catalyst for him to receive a major psychological and spiritual healing. By releasing his crippling guilt and grief from the accident, his longstanding depression and suicidal thoughts gave way to joy. The healing also extended to his mother who felt a lifting of the emotional burdens she had been carrying for her son. Both mother and son left that night with radiant faces. It would be the last time I would see the young man. A few years later I found out that he had died in an accident at home. He was not physically healed by our prayer, but his healing was much greater. He encountered Jesus and through that rediscovered his own true identity in communion with the Beloved Son.

Through prayer we can help others encounter Jesus's love, he will take it from there

Pray for them to encounter Jesus

Love → How is loving non st got to do with Play?

stop

Do we believe

Identity crashed out of love & furlow

THE BELOVED SON

We are not the sum of our weaknesses and failures; we are the sum of the Father's love for us and our real capacity to become the image of his Son.

Pope John Paul II,
World Youth Day 2002

How do you perceive yourself? Do you see yourself as the sum of all your weaknesses and failures, or the image of the beloved son? Do you believe you are cherished and deeply lovable or inherently worthless and easily discarded? Is your fundamental identity that of a sinner or a saint? Don't be too quick to answer these questions. You may believe one thing based on the way you have been taught but quite another in the way you really see yourself in the depths of your heart. And this is no small matter. What you believe about yourself in your heart becomes your identity, which in turn shapes everything in your life.

Before the Father, who is infinitely holy, we are all sinners in need of his mercy (Lk 18:13). But in the eyes of St. Paul and the Church, the baptized are called saints (with a small "s") and beloved children in Christ (Rom 1:7; Col 1:2; *CCC*, 1272). All of this can become rather confusing, can't it? The Church teaches that when we "put on Christ" at Baptism (Gal 3:27), we receive our new identity

Fear of loss — Friends

Isolation — Relationships

in Christ (*CCC*, 1265). The old is gone and the new has taken its place. So why then do we keep hanging on to our old identities, based in the accusations of the evil one? We may believe we are chosen and redeemed, but our lives often belie that fact. Just listen to the authoritative voice of the Church again: "Yet certain temporal consequences of sin remain in the baptized, such as suffering, illness, death, and such frailties inherent in life as weakness in character, and so on" (*CCC*, 1264). We are confused because we are living from two competing identities: we are beloved children of the Father but still find ourselves struggling with weaknesses of character and the consequences of sin that remain with us even after our Baptisms.

Jesus has no such inner conflicts or contamination of soul. His identity is clear and without confusion. For all eternity he is The Beloved Son of the Father, in communion with the Holy Spirit (*CCC*, 221).

The mystery of the Trinity and Jesus' eternal identity as Son is obviously beyond our capacity to fully comprehend with our reason. But as with any mystery of faith, we are called to contemplate and enter into it with ever greater degrees of illumination from the Holy Spirit. Sometimes images that convey the words of scripture are a great aid in this process. With that purpose in mind, we often employ a teaching tool in our conferences called "human sculpting."[1]

During this demonstration, three volunteers are chosen to represent the Trinity: one to be the Father, one to be the Son, and the third to represent the Holy Spirit. I assure the volunteers that they do not need to worry about offering an adequate image—this is totally impossible. I simply ask them to trust the Holy Spirit to guide them in the process and direct each of them to assume a posture in relation to the others, revealing an image of holy communion between the Father, Son, and Holy Spirit. Can you think of how you would portray this image of God's innermost mystery of love if you were one of the volunteers? Which member of the Trinity would you want to represent? How would you depict yourself in relation to the others?

I am often touched by the beautiful demonstrations each time, as are many of the participants. On one occasion, the person playing the Father opened his arms to the beloved Son, who responded with a bear hug and didn't let go for several minutes; in return, the Father embraced the Son with great affection. As they embraced, the Holy Spirit began dancing around them joyfully. On another occasion, the person playing the beloved Son kneeled before the Father (see Eph 3:14), while the person representing the Father reached out and placed his hand on the Son's head, blessing him; the Holy Spirit extended one arm to each, connecting the Father and Son in a bond of love.

As beautiful and moving as these images can be, they are still inadequate in expressing the glory of Jesus as beloved Son. They reveal the impression of the artists and sculptors, who are limited by their faith and prayer life. We are careful not to represent "vain images" of God (Ex 20:4) and test all these creative expressions in light of the truth revealed in scripture. That is why starting with imagery revealed in scripture can be most trustworthy.

One of the most beautiful images of Jesus as beloved Son comes from the Gospel of Luke, when Jesus is entering into the Jordan River to be baptized by John the Baptist. Allow your heart to enter in, as you listen to the Father blessing his Son from heaven, and then watch in your imagination as the Holy Spirit descends upon the beloved Son:

> After all the people had been baptized and Jesus also had been baptized and was praying, heaven was opened and the Holy Spirit descended upon him in bodily form like

a dove. And a voice came from heaven, "You are my be-loved Son; with you I am well pleased." (Lk 3:21–22)

Can you envision yourself on the side of the Jordan watching this scene unfold? Notice that before Jesus accomplishes anything, the Father expresses unconditional love and delight in his Son. The Father's approval is not based on Jesus' performance. Rather, he delights in Jesus because of *who he is*. Those of us who have children and grandchildren can relate, at least in a small measure, to the Father's unconditional love for his son. When I look at my children, grandchildren, and spiritual children, my heart often swells with love. I delight in each of them and treasure each of them for who they are, individually and uniquely. Though I enjoy seeing their accomplishments, it is not the foundation of my love for them. How much more the Father freely delights in his beloved Son. Can you even begin to comprehend the Father's love for Jesus? I can almost see and hear the Father looking down from heaven and saying to all who will listen, "This is my son. I delight in him. He brings great joy to my heart."

Our Faith teaches us that at Baptism we were united with Jesus as Beloved Son. This too is hard for us to comprehend, but we are invited by the Holy Spirit to contemplate this mystery. Not long ago I observed as Neal Lozano invited a roomful of seminarians to enter into the scene of Jesus' Baptism in prayer, as a way of bringing home the reality that we became united with Jesus at our Baptisms.[2] Are you open to trying this together right now?

- Picture yourself, with the eyes of your heart, standing in the river with Jesus.

- Imagine what it feels like as you are brought down into the water with him.

- Now as you ascend again from the water, realize that a miracle has taken place: Jesus is in you, and you are in him.

- That means the Father's words are for you: "This is my beloved son (or daughter) with whom I am well pleased." How do you feel when the Father speaks those words to you?

- As the Holy Spirit descends upon you, he anoints you with wisdom, knowledge, faith, and many gifts, including gifts of healing (1 Cor 12:8–10). He fills your spirit with love, joy, peace, kindness, and the other manifestations of his presence (Gal 5:22–23). *I can and have healed !*

- You are now united with Jesus.

- I encourage you to pause now and allow this experience to become real to you in prayer. Notice that it was during prayer, following his Baptism, that Jesus was able to see heaven open. All of us, since our Baptisms, have a similar kind of access to heaven through prayer. Remember St. Paul's and St. John's experiences of seeing heavenly realities? (See 2 Cor 12:1–5; Rv 1:9–20.) We can do the same.

Heavenly Father, please speak to our hearts and allow us to know that, in Jesus, we are your beloved children in whom you delight. Stir into flame the gift of the Holy Spirit that you have placed within each of us, filling us with your love, joy, and strength and taking away our fear (1 Tm 1:6–7). We ask this in union with your beloved Son, Jesus. Amen.

[handwritten notes]

Lauren — If a friend asks, say my mom + dad so love this future a police...

Love binds us and helps us accept the other as they are without judgment. We display the flag out of love for the police who protect us, sacrifice their life for us. Let our love be enough...

When you identified with Jesus at his Baptism, did you believe the Father delights in you with the same pleasure he has when he looks at Jesus? I don't have any trouble believing the Father delights in Jesus. Why wouldn't he? Jesus is perfect. He does everything the Father wants him to do. He is God. But when it comes to seeing myself as a beloved son of the Father, I am not nearly as confident. I am flawed; I don't do everything the Father commands me to do. I am far from perfect, despite pretending to be sometimes. Can you relate? Do you see how quickly we go back to our performance and shame, rather than trusting the covenant relationship we have with the Father through our Baptisms?

There is so much in us that doubts whether the Father really loves and delights in us. No matter how many times we read passages of scripture that assure us that the Father loves us with every bit of love that he has for Jesus (e.g., Jn 15–17), we still find it difficult to let it sink in. My experience of the Father's love back in the chapel at Christ Renews His Parish (CRHP) changed my life forever. I felt as if I was going to burst with joy. But even now, on many days, I find it hard to believe that the Father really delights in *me*. Over and over again, I need to be reminded of these realities and am grateful that the Father desires to remind me often.

Just recently, a member of our prayer team sent me this from Pope Francis's homily on the feast of the Sacred Heart of Jesus: "The Lord loves us tenderly. . . . He does not love us with words. He comes close . . . and gives us His love with tenderness." He continues on to acknowledge the struggle we have in receiving his love: "This is really very difficult: letting ourselves be loved by Him."[3] Hearing the faith struggles of many over the years, I realize I am not alone in finding it difficult to receive God's love. How easily we fall back into that old "God the taskmaster mentality," the one I thought I completely shed in the chapel during CRHP. Our fallen human nature wants to continually bring us back into "a spirit of slavery to fall back into fear." In doing so, we deny the reality that as his beloved children we have "received a spirit of adoption" by which we can call God our Abba (Daddy) (Rom 8:15).

Which Son Are You?

and he has 7
— mom -ter) - farl)
— susan —
— Kids
— corer

When we received a "spirit of adoption" at our Baptisms, we were promised boundless treasures from the Father's storehouse. Jesus said all we have to do is ask because the Father delights in giving us good gifts (Lk 11:13). When we trust him, we can bring our desires and brokenness to the Father and allow ourselves to become vulnerable enough to receive the healing we need in our lives. In contrast, when we do not believe that we are the Father's beloved, we remain bound in "a spirit of slavery" borne out of fear. Rather than living in freedom in communion with Jesus, we spend our days under the constant oppression of sin and law.

When we do not believe that we are the Father's beloved, we remain bound in "a spirit of slavery" borne out of fear.

We become like one or both of the sons in Jesus' parable of the prodigal son (Lk 15:11–32). We either wind up like the older brother, who keeps trying to earn his Father's love and looks down on his brother, or we wind up as the younger one, who gives up trying to please the Father and indulges in a life of sin. Most of us start our healing journey identifying more with one son or the other. Which of the two "sons" do you relate to the most? Are you more like the dutiful son, trying to please the Father by being good enough to get his approval? Or are you more like the rebellious son, choosing instead to indulge in whatever will medicate your pain? Either way, trying to find life apart from the Father leaves us miserable and acting like orphans who have to beg for our spiritual food.[4] We have nowhere to go with our pain and unmet needs. Without a firm identity as beloved children, we end up living lives of moral perfectionism trying to please God (like me) or reckless abandon and self-indulgence (like my brother Dave).

In Henri Nouwen's brilliant reflection on the prodigal son story, he discovered elements of both sons in himself and invites us to do the same.[5] As our eyes are opened to face our brokenness, we too become aware that we can identify with both sons. They have much in common. Both remain blinded to the Father's unconditional love for them. Neither realizes that the Father is waiting with open arms to receive them. They both try to resolve their pain apart from the Father. One (the older brother) covers his hurt with performance and hides his sins; the other relieves his pain with addictions. Whether we are "rebels" or "rule keepers," we cannot shake the tentacles of pride and shame.

Do you recognize any of these identity beliefs in your life: I'm . . . bad, stupid, fat, ugly, lazy, unlovable, inadequate, or dirty?

Rebellious sons and daughters are more aware of their shame, finding it easier to identify with failures, weaknesses, and the messages coming from their wounded self-image. Do you recognize any of these identity beliefs in your life: I'm . . . bad, stupid, fat, ugly, lazy, unlovable, inadequate, or dirty? The list goes on. Even if these specific labels don't fit us personally, each one of us has our own litany of self-sabotaging accusations. Those who are more like the rebellious prodigal may exhibit self-hatred outwardly by indulging in all manner of self-destructive behavior. Wearing shame as a garment, rebellious sons and daughters cover up their deeper pride behind a mask of self-hatred.

Those of us who identify more with the older brother cover our shame with the pride of our achievements and accolades.[6] We find our identity in self-righteousness and self-reliance. Though our wounded hearts are just like those of our self-loathing counterparts, we put on a respectable face to the world around us. Even our religious practices can become part of our false front. When it comes right down to it, as John Eldredge is fond of pointing out, we all become "posers" in one way or another.[7] While denying the glory of God in us, we instead choose the cheap counterfeit, vainglory. Yet this is the last thing we want to admit to ourselves or to anyone else for that matter.

Underneath all our masks and escapes, both sons remain controlled by a servile fear of God, leading each to run away and hide from "God the taskmaster." Whether we outwardly thumb our nose at him or more respectably numb our hearts by constantly striving to please him, we still remain distant from him.

Jesus told this story of the prodigal son and similar parables (see Lk 15:1–3) not only to reveal the Father's love but also to expose the religious pride of the Pharisees and other leaders, showing them that the shame-filled sinners and tax collectors were running to him first. Notice their reaction. They wanted to kill him rather than face their own brokenness and their need for a savior. They chose control rather than vulnerability and thus remained blinded by their pride. Rather than see themselves as revelations of the Father's glory in the beloved Son, they chose vainglory instead.

Lest we become too quick to judge them, we need to examine ways we are prone to fall into a similar trap. As I examine my life, particularly before the healing encounters with Jesus in my early thirties, I recognize myself in the older brother syndrome; I covered my sin and brokenness behind all my accomplishments. I kept trying to earn the Father's love. These words from Deacon Jim Keating, who teaches at the Institute for Priestly Formation, described my condition well for many years: "If he does not receive this identity [as beloved son] and come to savor and contemplate it, the man will make decisions that reflect a search for the Father's love, rather than make decisions in the light of such love."[8]

Before coming to know my identity in Jesus as beloved Son, I was constantly striving to be good enough for the Father but never feeling as if I measured up. Remember the blasphemy I spoke in my heart: "What in the hell is so good about God?" That sprang from believing the lie that I had to measure up to God's standards before I was lovable. Though a son of God, I was still living under the law and coming up short (see Jas 2:10). When I failed to measure up, the enemy then accused me of my failures. My wounds of abandonment and rejection were all mixed in there too. To make matters worse, I was (and still am to some degree) projecting my standards onto others, judging and unconsciously rejecting them for not measuring up. The movie *Good Will Hunting* helped me see it all more clearly, but only God's grace is able to bring me into complete freedom from this self-righteous bondage.

Through it all, I remained blinded by my pride as I hid my brokenness behind various talents and accomplishments. I took on various identities based in performance: Bob the good student, the star athlete, the responsible older brother, the Christian. I repressed most of what was not consistent with this image, including my broken heart and deviant behavior. When I later earned my doctorate, I added more layers of insulation, becoming the good teacher and wise therapist, and still not really facing my deeper heart in an honest way. It was easier to teach others and help them face their brokenness than it was to face my own.

Gods Grace gives us
Freedom to love

A constructed persona like this develops over a lifetime, but I can remember the specific day it began to take hold in my life in a substantial way. The defining moment occurred at the end of eighth grade, four months after Dad left. We were still living in our home in Bethel Park, Pennsylvania. Almost overnight I noticed that I looked and felt more like a man. My newly developed muscular body was a far cry from the skinny un-affirmed boy I was less than a year before. More than that, I was now the "man of the house," helping care for my younger brothers and sisters, and believing I could console my heartbroken mother.

The crystallizing event itself was rather insignificant, though the effect was substantial. As I mindlessly ambled down the basement stairs leading to my bedroom, I overheard Mom talking on the phone to one of her close friends. Mom's words, spoken with exuberance and pride, caught my attention: "My son Bob made the all-stars in three sports." To this day, I find it very difficult to describe my internal reaction. As I try to put myself back in the situation, my emotions are oddly conflicting. On one hand, I felt as proud as a peacock. Having been publicly crowned a great athlete, I was now a person worthy of being adored and glorified. On the other hand, I felt disgusted knowing that something about this was not only idolatrous but also displaced.

In the face of all our family shame and devastation, this was one of many small attempts (false as they were) to restore our family pride. Though I still struggled internally the next year, it wouldn't take long before I suppressed the rest of my shame and hurt, hiding it behind this image of being the "star." Losing sight of my true identity as beloved son of the Father, and not wanting to face the feelings of rejection and abandonment by my earthly father, I chose the easy way out. I quit worshipping God in the midst of my brokenness and vainly worshipped myself instead. I exchanged the glory of God for vainglory.

Vainglory, a weakness of our fallen nature, grows stronger when we refuse to face our brokenness. It is a futile attempt to find life in and through ourselves instead. Vainglory brings death to our hearts, blinding our eyes to the truth. We worship ourselves in self-idolatry and avoid intimacy with the Father.

God's glory is the antithesis of vainglory. As St. Irenaeus is renowned for proclaiming, "The glory of God is man fully alive." Only when we are fully alive in Christ are we capable of beholding our dignity as beloved children of the Father. Pope John Paul II understood this reality well and boldly proclaimed the message to the whole world throughout the years he shepherded the universal Church. We began this chapter with his quote from World Youth Day in Toronto: "We are the sum of the Father's love for us and our real capacity to become the image of his Son." We are *not* the sum of our weaknesses and failures. Neither are we the sum of our achievements and successes or religious practices. No, we are much more than all these things. We are beloved children of the Father (1 Jn 2:7, 3:1).

Intimacy with Jesus

Intimacy with Jesus, the beloved Son, leads us into an ever-growing knowledge of ourselves as the Father's beloved. "Jesus Christ fully reveals man . . . to himself and makes his supreme calling clear."[9] Jesus is the real "star" of the human race. You and I are created to reflect *his* glory (2 Cor 3:18). Jesus is the only person worthy of our full adulation. And yet, his entire life was marked by humility, not vainglory. He came to earth as a baby, grew up in a family, and endured the trials and tribulations of life and death that are an inherent part of this broken world. He did not run from brokenness, but in humility he fully took on our brokenness with the greatest possible vulnerability.

And this is the rub: To be fully conformed to the image of the beloved Son we must humble ourselves and follow in Jesus' footsteps all the way through the Cross and into the Resurrection. We all have to die in order to live. Isn't this the heart of the Gospel message? St. Paul emphasized this over and over again in his preaching: "For I resolved to know nothing . . . except Jesus Christ, and him crucified" (1 Cor 2:2). He was moved to tears lamenting all the false presentations of the Gospel making its hearers "enemies of the cross of Christ" whose "glory is in their 'shame'" and whose "minds are occupied with earthly things" (Phil 3:18–19). I shudder at how much I have been an enemy of the Cross in my life, being more concerned about earthly things and self-survival, all the while avoiding the Cross, which is God's only path to true healing and salvation.

> *To be fully conformed to the image of the beloved Son we must humble ourselves and follow in Jesus' footsteps all the way through the Cross and into the Resurrection.*

The way to the Cross begins at Baptism, which itself is a symbol and reality of death and resurrection (Rom 5:3–4). Jesus walking into the waters of the Jordan began his first steps along the way to Calvary. Jesus fully lived his identity as "beloved Son" all the way to the cross, deeply pleasing the Father in this way. Pope Benedict XVI affirms all this in *Jesus of Nazareth*: "Baptism is an acceptance of death for the sins of humanity, and the voice that calls out 'This is my beloved Son' over the baptismal waters is an anticipatory reference to the Resurrection."[10]

I don't know about you, but I have lived much of my life in fear of the Cross, running from it, rather than embracing it. I don't like to suffer, and I also don't like to let anyone else tell me how to live. I want to be my own person. The problem with "doing it my way," as Frank Sinatra sang many years ago, is that it makes me an enemy of the cross of Christ. Even as I acknowledge this, it hurts. Running from suffering has never brought me into resurrection life. The good news is that the Holy Spirit always finds a way to break through my fears and defenses. Once again he used another Hollywood movie, *What about Bob?* Are you surprised that I would be impacted by another movie about a therapist and counselee? It is rather humorous and predictable, isn't it?

This time, I immediately identified with the character of the therapist, Dr. Leo Marvin, played by Richard Dreyfuss. In the opening scene, we learn that his bestselling book has recently been published and he is taking a much-needed break to go on vacation with his family. There's only one problem: he can't get away from his patient Bob, who is played by the ridiculously funny Bill Murray. Bob idolizes Marvin and can't live without him. His unhealthy dependence leads him to follow Dr. Marvin and his family on vacation.

Not able to get away from Bob, Dr. Marvin grows to detest this vulnerable man he once offered to help. After many attempts to get free from Bob's omnipresence, Dr. Marvin loses his composure and develops a plan to kill Bob. Buying enough dynamite to blow up a city, he ties Bob up in the woods and lights the fuse. Bob, already a fearful person, is now terrified. But at the edge of death, he recalls the lessons from Dr. Marvin's book *Baby Steps* and doesn't panic. One baby step at a time, he finds a way to get free before the dynamite explodes.

When Bob finally emerges from the woods, he is a free man. No longer bound by a fear of death (Heb 2:15), he is able to love for the first time in his life. Fully healed of his fearful neuroses, he reveals the glory of God, "a man fully alive." In the end, he is even more grateful and indebted to Dr. Marvin for saving him, which infuriates Leo all the more. Like many of us in the helping professions, Dr.

Marvin had more knowledge than freedom. Despite all his clinical expertise, his patient Bob ends up being the one who knows the reality of healing. As a result, Dr. Marvin hates Bob, much like the Pharisees detested Jesus for exposing their hypocrisy. Meanwhile, Dr. Marvin's family fully embraces the lovable and carefree Bob, so much so that Bob eventually marries Marvin's sister. When Bob later becomes a psychologist himself, he writes a bestseller as did his mentor. You might have already guessed the title: *Death Therapy*. To add insult to injury, Bob dedicated the book to Dr. Leo Marvin.

With all its silliness, and probably because of the character Bob's childlikeness, the Holy Spirit spoke to me powerfully through this movie. Though I started the movie identifying with Dr. Marvin, I ended it by rediscovering the childlike Bob in me. It was as if through the entire movie the Father was asking me, What about Bob? What about that lovable and at times fearful kid you shoved away behind your therapist persona?

Remember how I took on the role of "family therapist" as a teenager, covering my fears and insecurities? Taking on all that responsibility and hiding behind my ego and accomplishments not only wore me out but also disconnected my heart from God. I lost sight of the lovable Bob who is the real me. No wonder my family bought *What about Bob?* T-shirts for my fiftieth birthday party. They want the real childlike me too, just as Leo Marvin's family was more attracted to Bob than to Dr. Marvin.

I now realize that the way of the Cross—Jesus' "death therapy"—is the only way to get free from self-idolatry and the underlying fearfulness that has kept me bound in my false identities, so that I can live from my true identity as beloved son. This is true for each one of us in our own way. Each of us has developed a false identity to cover our brokenness.

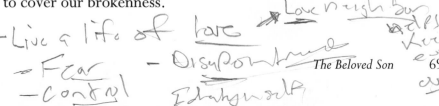

Take a moment to consider how you may have hidden and buried your true self.

- Are you like the prodigal son, identifying with your failures and weaknesses?

- Or do you find your identity in your accomplishments, like the older brother? *Later*

- Take a few moments and write out the "false identities" in your life.

- What fears and insecurities are hidden behind these false identities?

- Describe yourself as a carefree and secure child. What were you like? If you can't remember, what would it look like now for you to be childlike and secure in the Father's love?

Jesus came to "proclaim liberty to captives" (Lk 4:18) and to show us how to live from our true identity as beloved children. Jesus' death therapy is the only way this is accomplished. Our false self must be crucified with him, so that our true identity as his beloved can shine forth in glory. This is our healing journey, which requires both courage and humility in facing our brokenness.

I am = Son of god
- Friend
- Uncle
- Leader
- Mentor
- Father
- Husband
-

Death Therapy
- Power of Prayer
Can heal
can save
can change lives

PART TWO
FACING OUR BROKENNESS

The Devil may try to use the hurts of life and sometimes our own mistakes to make you feel it is impossible that Jesus really loves you.

Blessed Mother Teresa of Calcutta,
Letter to the Missionaries of Charity Family

CHAPTER FIVE

THE WHOLE PERSON
PERSPECTIVE

*Whoever wishes to heal man must see him in his whole-
ness and must know that his ultimate healing can only
be God's love.*

Pope Benedict XVI,
Jesus of Nazareth

Over the past few years, seeing God do amazing things in the lives of
many people, I began to expect that everyone I prayed with would be
healed. Then, I was confronted with seemingly "hopeless" situations,
where people had tried everything and could find no relief. Three
of these people have been suffering with debilitating depression for
many years. Their lives have been a living hell, and their families
have paid a heavy price, in every way. Before my interactions with
them, each one had been hospitalized for long periods of time and
had been given extensive treatment by reputable medical personnel.
Their treatments included many kinds of antidepressant medicines,
state-of-the-art therapies, and when nothing else worked, multiple
electroshock treatments to destroy brain cells. When I heard what
they had gone through, my heart broke for them and their families.

I have no reason to doubt the quality of care these people received or the competence of their caregivers. They went to the best hospitals and were given the best possible care these institutions could provide. I would venture to guess that most of those caregivers had more expertise and training in the diagnosis and treatment of depression than I did. But training, in a traditional scientific worldview, can sometimes blind good, caring people and disable them from facilitating true and lasting healing. Science by its very nature analyzes and dissects everything into parts. Within that framework, people are defined by their symptoms and the parts of their body or soul that aren't functioning properly.

In most medical and psychological environments, people are not fully seen as whole persons but rather are identified by their diagnoses. While one could argue that scientific diagnoses have an important role in treatment, I would counter that they can also be problematic because they amplify the symptom and often deny the underlying disease. Psychological diagnoses too easily slide into personal identities, all but obliterating our true identity as beloved children of the Father. How many times have you heard the phrase "She is bipolar" or "He is narcissistic" as if the diagnoses defines the person? Labels such as these rarely bring out our compassion and more often lead us to fear and judge the person and distance ourselves from them. At least that has been my experience.

That is only one of many problems with the traditional scientific worldview. Since the vast majority of doctors, nurses, psychologists, and therapists have been trained in this mechanistic approach, we have a tendency to treat symptoms more than people. As a result we are more often taught to alleviate the symptoms, without attending to the underlying causes. There are obviously exceptions to this rule, and these exceptions seem to be on the rise; but in general, as I hear the histories of people who have suffered for years, my heart breaks for all the ways their deeper hurts have been overlooked. This is not an issue of superior approaches. It is a matter of reclaiming our Christian and Catholic worldview in our approach to healing.

Do you know what the word *catholic* means? According to the *Catechism of the Catholic Church*, it literally means "'according to the totality' or 'in keeping with the whole'" (*CCC*, 830). Catholic theology sees all reality, including all that has been broken and fragmented by sin, within a broader reality of "wholeness." Similarly, the word *Christian* means "belonging to Christ" or "follower of Christ." As followers of Christ, we claim to believe he is our healer, the "physician of our souls and bodies" (*CCC*, 1509).

Putting those two definitions together provides a Catholic Christian worldview of healing and wholeness: Jesus Christ came to restore everything that has been broken by the ravages of sin. He promises to fully restore all things into their intended wholeness. His redemption brings healing for the whole person, the whole family, the whole church, the whole world, and even as St. Paul assures us, the whole universe (see Rom 8:18–25; Eph 4:1–6).

Again I want to emphasize, I am not discrediting science, medicine, or psychology. They have their place in the world of healing. But as a culture we have bought into seeing reality from a materialist perspective. Without allowing the Gospel to inform us, this scientific and professional worldview is limited and distorting. Science can build on the knowledge of faith, but it cannot replace it without serious consequences.[1] Our Catholic faith, centered in the person of Jesus Christ, provides a unique perspective that brings hope and allows us to see all brokenness in light of God's vision for wholeness.

In practice, most of us approach our own healing as if we were secular atheists. We have been so influenced by science that we view ourselves and our diseases from a "fragmented" perspective. We act as though our symptoms are the problem and look for the quickest and easiest way to alleviate our suffering. In the end, we wonder why we do not receive the healing we long for.

How many people do you know who have been prescribed medication for one symptom that only caused three more symptoms, requiring three more medications? We may laugh at the concept, but the reality is not very funny for those who are suffering the side effects. This is a serious issue in symptom-driven care and a reflection of the larger problem in our world. We have become like the proverbial blind men examining an elephant. We do not see the whole elephant but instead become experts at describing the parts.

Let's step back a minute and take a look at the bigger picture. What do you believe was in God's mind when he created human beings? What was our condition before sin entered the world (Gn 1–3)? These very questions inspired Pope John Paul II as a philosopher and theologian. His writings reveal great insight into the dignity of our humanity: the Father created us to share in the intimate communion of love that he enjoys with his Son and the Holy Spirit.[2] Simply stated, we were created out of love and for love. Love is the origin and destiny of our lives. "Our lives are senseless without love."[3]

In the beginning of creation, Pope John Paul II informs us, everything existed in communion and harmony, in submission to the Father.[4] There was no suffering, sickness, disease, or death. There were no conflicts, wars, hatred, or murder. We did not have any psychological or spiritual maladies. God's love kept everything in unity. Communing with the Triune God, with one another, and with nature, our spirits maintained their harmony with God's Spirit, which in turn kept us fully integrated in body, soul, and spirit. We did not have to face the daily interior battle between "spirit" and "flesh" (Rom 8:5). All was one, integrated and whole, and operating the way God designed for us to live.

But when sin entered the world, everything fell apart; that which was once unified became fragmented, and the process of disintegration has been having its way ever since. As I learned in high school physics, apart from grace, the entire universe now tends toward disorder. Those areas originally designed for communion the cause of our greatest suffering. We all feel the pain of from God, with one another, and most vividly, within ourse..

The *Catechism of the Catholic Church* summarizes these effects of original sin with great clarity:

> The harmony in which they [Adam and Eve] had found themselves, thanks to original justice, is now destroyed: the control of the soul's spiritual faculties over the body is shattered; the union of man and woman becomes subject to tensions, their relations are thenceforth marked by lust and domination. Harmony with creation is broken . . . death makes its entrance into human history. (*CCC*, 400)

In that short account of the consequences of sin in the world, we are able to see the underlying roots of all of our diseases. The primary root of our suffering and sickness is separation from God, resulting in the fragmentation of our bodies and souls, and thus manifesting in broken relationships with other people and nature. This is the ultimate cause of our daily angst. But we can all breathe a collective sigh of relief, because the story does not end with sin and brokenness.

Jesus came to redeem and restore all that is fragmented and separated in and around us, to bring everything back into the wholeness that God intended from the beginning. Christ's redemption restores what is broken and brings it progressively back into unity. This is why Pope Benedict XVI says that "healing is the entire content of our redemption when understood at a sufficiently deep level."[5] You may wonder, as I do, what this "sufficiently deep level" refers to. As I've reflected on this, I believe it entails the five primary areas that have been broken by original sin and are thus in need of healing[6]:

1. relationship between us and God (spiritual)
2. relationship between us and others (relational)
3. integration within us: soul and spirit (psychological)
4. integration within us: body and soul (physical)
5. relationship between us and nature (ecological)

Can you think of any infirmity, disease, or psychological malady that is not rooted in one or more of these five primary relationships that define our lives? And yet they are not really five separate areas; they are all intimately interconnected, and part of a larger whole. The problem with our modern world, and especially with our scientific approaches to healing, is that we too often see them all separately. We go to pastors, priests, and rabbis for spiritual healing; to marriage and family therapists and social workers for relational healing; to psychologists and psychiatrists for psychological healing; to medical doctors and physical therapists for physical healing; and to environmentalists and nutritionists for ecological healing.

And even within those divisions, we further compartmentalize. For example, think of all the different medical specialties: urology, gynecology, endocrinology, and the list goes on. Can you see the problem? It is not that we have all these specialties. Fields of specialization are of great benefit as long as those in the specialty areas have an understanding of how everything fits together. A few anatomy courses or a course on psychology are not enough. We end up offering nothing more than relief of symptoms that in the long run will only bring about more and different symptoms.

In order to be instruments of healing for others as well as find our own healing, we need to see the whole picture of our humanity in light of God's divinity. This is the point St. Paul makes about the unity of the body: "As a body is one though it has many parts, and all the parts of the body, though many, are one body, so also Christ. For in one Spirit we were all baptized into one body. . . . There are many parts, yet one body" (1 Cor 12:12–13a, 20). St. Paul, in considering both our human bodies as well as Christ's body, offers an authentic Catholic Christian worldview.

You may be wondering what happened to each of those people I mentioned earlier who were suffering with debilitating depressions. Well, the quick answer is they are all growing in hope and are engaged in the process of healing, though their healing journeys have been markedly different. One had a significant breakthrough and is continuing to heal; another is in the process of a long and progressive healing, while the third is only beginning the process of identifying the underlying issues of her depression. But in each case, when they moved from a "symptom" focus to a "whole person" perspective, they began to experience genuine hope. Since hopelessness is often the driving force in depression, this is no small matter.

Even though they were each being treated in similar ways in their respective hospital environments, their particular root issues were different. The first woman discovered that her depression was rooted in un-grieved abandonment pain from when she was given up for adoption as a baby. When the Holy Spirit revealed this to her, she was able to release the trauma she had been carrying all her life. She was spontaneously and immediately healed of her depression symptoms and able to receive God's love in the depths of her heart for the first time. But more than that, she was also instantly healed of fibromyalgia, a painful condition of the muscles, joints, tendons, and so forth, that results in chronic fatigue, which had plagued her for many years.

Even more amazing to both of us was the immediate healing of her son's "untreatable" physical ailment, at the exact moment she was being set free of her symptoms, though he was in a different city at the time. He had not been able to find any relief for his problem until then. Now, try to explain their healing with medical science. The Divine Physician knew the source of the mother's depression and he also knew how the physical, psychological, and generational issues were all interconnected. He alone knew what this woman needed as well as her son, who somehow mysteriously carried his mother's distress in his own body and soul. Yes I know, for many of us this is hard to believe. But it is true.

I spoke to the second woman over the phone, from her hospital bed. She was approaching her one-year mark at the hospital with little apparent progress. Her husband spent most of every day sitting by her bedside. Within a few minutes of prayer and listening, we discovered that her depression started when her children left home. When we stopped to pray together again about the deeper root issues, the Holy Spirit immediately brought her attention to her mother's death, when this woman was a young girl around the age of ten. Finally knowing the cause of her depression was greatly relieving to her, though she was not yet ready to face her grief. Discovering the cause of her depression encouraged her significantly, as well as her husband and family. With her newfound understanding, she had hope again. A light was beginning to shine in the darkness of her despair, and the yearlong battle with medications, electroshock therapy, and endless days of hospitalization had an end in sight.

One of the saddest situations involved a man who had been chronically depressed off and on for over forty years. His parents had both committed suicide when he was in his early twenties, leaving him in a daily battle for his own life. He had tried everything the healthcare system had to offer. With a strong medical background, he researched the best solutions but found little more than temporary relief. Despite all his struggles, Jesus continued to sustain this man in faith and eventually led him to a Christian hospital/retreat center that focused on the spiritual roots of physical and mental illness. During the week there, this man faced many layers of un-forgiveness toward himself, his parents, and his wife. By the end of the week, his depression lifted considerably after he forgave his parents and his wife. But his self-hatred was the hardest thing for him to deal with.

Since returning home, he is still working through that issue and guarding against falling back into his old thought patterns. In prayer, he has come to discover a deeper root issue to his depression and self-hatred. At the age of two, he was struck in the face by his father during a fit of rage. He continues to work toward complete healing of this underlying source of his pain, though it remains well-guarded. To date he has not been able to access the trauma that is contained in those early memories. On most days, he wants to live rather than die. He is not yet where he wants to be but is in a much better frame of mind than he was before.

As different as these three examples appear, they actually have much in common. After years of searching for answers, all three people received healing or the hope for healing when they faced their deep roots of brokenness. They were much like the woman in the gospels who had suffered without relief for twelve years and "spent her whole livelihood on doctors and was unable to be cured by anyone" (Lk 8:43). Like her, each of these three sufferers found their hope and healing through an encounter with Jesus.

There were other similarities between these three sufferers as well. Until now they had all been treated symptomatically, but their deeper healing and hope came when the underlying cause of their depression was addressed. In each case, healing simultaneously touched psychological, relational, and spiritual root issues that manifested in physical symptoms, supporting the Church's view that "spirit and matter in man are not two natures, but rather their union forms a single nature" (CCC, 365).

Pause for a moment to consider the nature of any ailments you carry.

- Is there some area where you have suffered without relief? Where did you turn for help?

- Do you have any insight about where this ailment may be rooted in physical, psychological, spiritual, environmental, or relational sources?

- Ask the Holy Spirit to show you more about these root issues.

Science is slowly beginning to understand and substantiate what the Church has known for ages. Many experts today agree that about 90 to 95 percent of all illnesses are "stress related."[7] Notice the similarity between the words *distress* and *disease*. Any area where our souls and bodies are not living in communion with God's Spirit is an area of dis-*ease*, which causes us to become dis-*stressed*, that is, not at peace within ourselves.

The roots may go deep into our childhood, as with the woman who was traumatized as an infant in her adoption; or they may go even deeper into the generations of the family, like the man whose parents committed suicide. Ultimately for all of us, the roots of our maladies go back even farther, to the fall of mankind. Living in this fallen world, we each have areas where our lives lack love, joy, and peace. Born into a culture that resists God's love and truth, we were set up for *disease* and *disintegration*.

With a renewed interest in the spiritual and psychological roots of illnesses, many healthcare practitioners and those in the psychological sciences are adopting holistic and functional approaches to treatment. These approaches have been around for years but were considered alternative and unscientific until recently. They are becoming increasingly mainstream now that science and practice are validating their greater effectiveness. Unfortunately, many of these holistic approaches to healing do not go far enough. Many are based in alternative spiritualities that deny the reality or divinity of Jesus Christ; in the end, this leads to more disintegration. By denying Jesus, the physician of our souls and bodies, they ignore the very source of our healing.

Years ago, I was treated by a kind and gifted state-licensed massage therapist, who I later discovered operated from a pantheistic worldview. She believed that "God" and the "universe" were synonymous and that Jesus was only one of many wise men. Understanding the interconnections of body, soul, and spirit, she was able to facilitate a level of healing in her patients. Over time, she gave me many books to read, and for the most part, they contained truth consistent with my Christian faith and experience as a therapist. However, as I continued to read some of these books, I began to notice a spiritual darkness descend upon me. Though they contained useful information about health and the integration of body and soul, the underlying spirituality was terribly misguided.

Unwittingly, I was being led into false worship. Under the guise of a pantheistic worldview, I was subtly encouraged to rely on myself rather than God, which only further enhanced my pride and vainglory. It was clearly not Christian, and it eventually had negative consequences in my life. Remember the hellish feeling I described on that Friday night of Christ Renews His Parish (CRHP), before my powerful encounter with the Holy Spirit the next night? That all began when I renounced the demonic spiritual influences behind those books.

After that, as much as I valued my massage therapist as a person, I knew I needed to find a Christian who could incorporate healing prayer with a reliance on Jesus Christ. Since then, I have only gone to therapists and doctors who incorporate healing prayer in their treatment. My medical doctor, dentist, chiropractor, and massage therapist are people who incorporate prayer in their life and practice. Spiritually, it has made a world of difference in my life.

❧

As Christians, we need to restore healthcare to its proper origins. This is only fitting, as the Church has always been involved in the care of the sick and in their restoration to wholeness. This is the conclusion of Dr. Harold Koenig, founder of the Center for the Study of Religion/Spirituality and Health at Duke University. His extensive research on the interconnection of spiritual and physical healing has led him to the realization that the Church has always been involved in caring for the health needs of people and has applied prayer along with science to bring restoration and healing. In addition to his extensive teaching and writing, Dr. Koenig is also a practicing physician who integrates healing prayer in his medical practice.[8]

There are many exciting developments in the field of healthcare practice and education, where spiritually minded practitioners see the bigger picture of how body, soul, and spirit are integrated within a context of relationships and ecology. Any casual search on the Internet or in the bookstore will reveal many good resources. One example is the work of J. Brennan Mullaney, a Catholic therapist I discovered a few years back. His book *Authentic Love* offers a reinterpretation of physical and psychological illness from a strictly Christian worldview. His diagnosis of our various health problems reveals great insight: "The avoidance, rejection, or deprivation of love is the source of all functional (physical, psychological, and spiritual) illness."[9] Do you realize how radical a statement that is in the world of healthcare? To attribute all our functional health concerns to a single cause, such as the deprivation of love, sounds ridiculously simple. But before you dismiss it too quickly, consider applying that to the three people I mentioned suffering from debilitating depressi. Their problems began with a traumatic loss of love, and the manifestations were not just psychological but also physical.

Mullaney's insights into the source of our healing are equally compelling, ring true to experience, and are validated by the preponderance of research on the efficacy of various forms of psychotherapy. This is what he says: "Love heals. Healing is an integral part of human love. Where love is, healing is constantly occurring."[10] Isn't this what Pope Benedict XVI is saying in *Jesus of Nazareth*? "Whoever wishes to heal man must see him in his wholeness and must know that his ultimate healing can only be God's love."[11]

We are created for love. Love allows us to grow as God intended, in wholeness and health. Without love, we get sick and become further disintegrated in body, soul, and spirit. Even our past experiences of being cut off from love can cause great stress on us mentally, emotionally, and physically, and thereby eventually manifest in illnesses of various kinds. Do you see how Brennan Mullaney's viewpoint has a lot of merit? Deprivation of love is the root of our disease—robbing us of peace and causing disintegration. Love, on the other hand, is the source of our healing and wholeness.

TAKE A MOMENT

Take a moment to consider how you view people and their illnesses.

- Do you define people by their brokenness, judging them by labels that define their behavior or symptoms, or do you see them in their wholeness?

- Do you believe that disease and dysfunction result from love deprivation? Why or why not?

- Do you believe that love heals? Explain why or why not.

Following the example of Brennan Mullaney and others like him, we need more Christians to develop anthropologies and treatment approaches that are faithful to scripture and Church teaching. If we will spend time in prayer and listen, we will begin to receive inspiration from heaven. I know this from experience. While I was on an eight-day silent retreat, the Holy Spirit inspired a simple framework for looking at our wholeness in Christ and how this wholeness can be disrupted by sin. I had been searching for this understanding for years but could never fully find it in all my training in the social sciences. And yet this model fit perfectly with the best available perspectives on health and wholeness.[12] I will share these discoveries with you in our next chapter, "A Tree and Its Fruit."

1. Spiritual - me & god
2. Relationship me & others
3. ~~Body~~/mind soul & Holy Spirit
4. Body — soul & Body
5. Nature us & nature

Root of Illness is a disordered way of
Tired of life
Security — Grounded in love
Purity — Grounded in love
Maturity — fruit of Jesus
Purity —

CHAPTER SIX

A TREE AND ITS FRUIT

The tree of knowledge of good and evil [is a] symbol of the covenant with God broken in man's heart.

Pope John Paul II,
Man and Woman He Created Them

We observed in the previous chapter that true healing must go beyond addressing symptoms to reach the underlying root issues. Father Mark Toups, who teaches with me, often uses a visual aid to illustrate this point in our spiritual lives. He brings in an apple and a small tree, to demonstrate that our individual sins are symptoms of a deeper soul disease. (You may protest that apples don't grow on small trees, and you would be right, but you can imagine the difficulty of bringing in a big tree for this illustration.)

Father Mark proposes to the attentive students, "Suppose this apple is your sin. And every time you come to the Sacrament of Reconciliation, you bring in more apples, representing the same sins you confess over and over again. This is a good thing, as you are receiving absolution and a clear conscience. But these sins are symptoms of a deeper soul disease (the tree)." Inviting participation, Father Mark asks: "What happens if you pick an apple off a tree?" The students, right on cue, respond, "More grow back." Father Mark, having them right where he wants them, proceeds: "So how many apples have to be pulled off the tree before the apples are completely gone?" The students gladly respond, "All of them."

With anticipation mounting, Father Mark continues: "How long will the apples be gone?" Students: "Till more grow back." Father Mark: "How many of you can relate to that problem, when it comes to confessing your sins?" Most of the hands in the room go up. Father Mark, who has a flare for the dramatic and a great sense of humor, then continues: "How do you get rid of these apples for good?" The response may come back quickly: "Cut down the tree." Father Mark responds, "Or better yet, pull the entire tree up from its roots." He has been known, on more than one occasion, at this point in the illustration, to pull the little tree up by its roots. When he does, dirt flies everywhere. Everyone laughs, except the cleaning service people and the arborists. The students get the point. Out of respect for those who are left with the cleanup, Father Mark now uses fake trees, or more often, just apples.

The tree illustration is not original to Father Mark or to our conferences. We are simply drawing the imagery from scripture and Church teaching. Throughout scripture, trees are used to illustrate the vitality of our spiritual life, representing one of two possible conditions. The "tree of life" is a symbol of our life in union with Christ, whereas the "tree of knowledge of good and evil" represents our life cut off from God (Gn 2:9). When in communion with God, we live from our true identity as his beloved children; when separated from him in ungodly self-reliance, we live from a false identity. There are no other options. Let's explore both of these trees in some depth, beginning with the tree of life.

The tree of life is a symbol of our communion with God, a life filled with virtue and good spiritual fruit (2 Pt 1:5–8; Gal 5:22–23). In scripture, we are first introduced to this imagery in the opening scenes of

Genesis where God is communing with Adam and Eve in the Garden of Eden (Gn 2:15–16). Psalm 1 gives the blueprint, painting a visual picture of those who trust in the Lord. They are "like a tree planted near streams of water that yields its fruit in season" (Ps 1:3). Jeremiah adds to the metaphor: "In the year of drought it shows no distress, but still bears fruit" (Jer 17:8). And Isaiah concludes, "They will be called oaks of justice, planted by the LORD to show his glory" (Is 61:3).

Continuing this theme in the New Testament, Jesus tells us plainly that a good tree comes from good seed, planted in good soil (Mt 13:24). This tree "does not bear rotten fruit" (Lk 6:43) but instead bears good "fruit that will remain" (see Jn 15:1–16). This fruit is none other than "the fruit of the Spirit": love, joy, peace, patience, kindness, and so forth (Gal 5:22–23). The tree-of-life symbolism culminates in the book of Revelation as John describes life in the heavenly city: "Then the angel showed me the river of life-giving water, sparkling like crystal, flowing from the throne of God and of the Lamb down the middle of its street. On either side of the river grew the tree of life that produces fruit twelve times a year, once each month; the leaves of the trees serve as medicine [healing] for the nations" (Rv 22:1–2).

Do you get the picture? The tree of life is a metaphor for our communion with Christ. This abiding relationship with Jesus is the source of our healing and bears the fruit of the Spirit. Jesus' love is the best medicine for our bodies, souls, and spirits. All of this became clear to me on my eight-day silent retreat. After an entire day of feeling the presence of the Holy Spirit as a burning sensation in my heart, I was awakened from sleep with three words: *security*, *maturity*, and *purity*. These three words proved to be a summation of our life in the Spirit.

Figure 6.1. Tree of life: security, maturity, and purity

PURITY
The fruit of love

MATURITY
Growth in love

SECURITY
Rooted and grounded in love

Some time later, I felt drawn to the book of Ephesians in the Bible and was surprised to see how these three words formed an outline for our life in Christ as members of God's family. Security is being "rooted and grounded in love" (Eph 3:17); maturity is growing into Christ-likeness, by increasing our capacity to love (Eph 4:7–16); and purity is the fruit of that love (Eph 5:1–5).

The alternative to the tree of life is "the tree of knowledge of good and evil," which according to Pope John Paul II represents God's covenant "broken in man's heart."[1] When our hearts are separated from God in ungodly self-reliance, we become filled with anxiety and *insecurity*, resulting in *immaturity* and bearing the bad fruit of *impurity* (Gal 5:19–21). Jeremiah describes this dead and fruitless tree with striking imagery: "Cursed is the man who trusts in human beings, who seeks his strength in flesh, whose heart turns away from the LORD. He is like a barren bush in the desert that enjoys no change of season, but stands in a lava waste, a salty and empty earth" (Jer 17:5–6).

Jeremiah's description seems pretty accurate to me; how about you? Have you ever felt as if you were a barren bush, in a dry desert where everything seemed an empty waste? That is what life is like when our roots are in ourselves, through ungodly self-reliance. Jesus builds on this description in the Sermon on the Plain: "A good tree does not bear rotten fruit, nor does a rotten tree bear good fruit. For every tree is known by its own fruit. For people do not pick figs from thornbushes, nor do they gather grapes from brambles" (Lk 6:43–44).

Jesus and Jeremiah are contrasting those who trust in God and flourish, and those who don't and wither away. But this imagery is not just about the redeemed and the unredeemed. It can also apply to specific areas in each one of our lives as followers of Christ. We are all engaged in a daily internal battle between what St. Paul refers to as "flesh" and "Spirit" (Rom 8:5–7; Gal 5:16–26; *CCC*, 2516). The "flesh" is rooted in ungodly self-sufficiency (tree of knowledge) whereas life in the Spirit refers to our abiding in Christ (tree of life).

Every thought and action in our life comes from one of these two invisible trees. Whatever we sow in our thought life will progressively manifest in our emotions, habits, and character (Gal 6:7–8). "Sow a thought, reap an action; sow an action, reap a habit; sow a habit, reap a character; sow a character and reap a destiny."[2] Little seeds become big trees if they aren't pulled up by their roots. We all carry around some barren bushes and deadly trees in our hearts.

The three Christians suffering from crippling depression mentioned in the last chapter illustrate our common dilemma. They are each Christians who at some level believe Jesus when he said, "I came so that they might have life and have it more abundantly" (Jn 10:10). Can you imagine their despair and self-doubt, wondering why they can't find this abundant life? Do you ever wonder where the joy is in your life? I sometimes do.

I can attest that each one of these dear sufferers, as much as they are capable, has a genuine trust in Jesus as their Redeemer. Each one of them prays and worships God regularly; yet each also has areas of his or her life that remain resistant to God's grace, due in large part to their unhealed wounds and un-repented sin. At least one of them harbored bitterness and self-hatred, but all three were deeply wounded as young children and responded to the trauma by closing their hearts to God in specific areas of their life. They did not do this intentionally or maliciously but as a form of survival and self-protection. Nevertheless, each of them became handicapped in their ability to feel secure and to give and receive love.

I know in my own life, even seemingly innocent attempts at self-preservation can too easily turn into ungodly self-reliance. My heart goes out to each of them in heartfelt compassion, giving me a small taste of Jesus' boundless compassion for them and each of us in the areas of our difficulty. But just as Jesus first forgave the sins of the paralytic before healing him (Mk 2:1–12), we need to be careful not to dismiss certain root attitudes of sin out of a false compassion for people. My experience tells me that unacknowledged sin frequently plays a part in our unhealed wounds and diseases of soul and body. That does not give us permission to judge the cause of another's illness, as Jesus made clear (Jn 9:2–3). Only God knows the depths of our hearts and the full cause of our infirmities.

Sin originates in the "father of lies" (Jn 8:44) and requires our consent before it can take root in our hearts (*CCC*, 1853). Once we let it in, it can destroy in us "what is essentially human."[3] Ordinarily, our sins begin as temptations from the evil one and then progress into our thoughts, words, and actions, manifesting as symptoms of a diseased heart (Mk 7:21). Each one of us harbors "evil" thoughts in our hearts, more often than we would like to admit. All of these diseased attitudes—hatred, gossip, bitterness, envy, pride, and fearfulness—and more can be concealed in our hearts for a long time. But eventually they manifest in our life in some way, affecting our health and well-being. When sins of the heart remain unseen and unaddressed, they eventually become deadly poisons to our bodies and souls.

We are all prone to these ungodly root attitudes, even when we are in grace-filled environments seeking God. Our mouths speak and our hearts believe much that is not like Jesus who is "full of grace and truth" (Jn 1:14). Because none of us has been fully conformed into the image of the Son, we are all subject to these works of the flesh. Remember my thoughts during the Sunday morning of the Christ Renews His Parish (CRHP) weekend. I was singing about God's goodness, but blasphemous thoughts came up from the depths of my heart. I didn't realize that sin lurked there in the darkness, until the strong presence of the Holy Spirit brought it into the light. My blasphemous thoughts actually revealed diseased attitudes of my heart, which grew out of the *Seven Deadly Sins*.

The Seven Deadly Sins

You may already be familiar with the seven deadly sins, as they have a long history in Church teaching. The phrase was actually coined in the sixth century by Pope Gregory the Great (*CCC*, 1866). But the ideas predate him to the earliest Christian times and before that with the Jewish people. The Desert Fathers played a key role in articulating these deadly sins in the centuries after Christ. Seeking earnestly to grow in holiness and understand their own hearts, they reflected carefully on the scriptures. With the aid of the Holy Spirit, they spent much time and thought applying what they were learning to the areas where they were struggling with sin. Eventually they were sought out by others for spiritual guidance. You could say they were the first spiritual directors and Christian therapists.[4]

By paying attention to the diseased attitudes within their hearts that kept cropping up, they began to see patterns that seemed universal. They called these diseased attitudes "capital sins" because they were the source of other sins. The phrase "deadly sins" eventually won out because it described the damaging effects of these familiar but lethal manifestations of the tree of knowledge of good and evil. Underneath all of these unhealthy attitudes they recognized a single root, "an inordinate love of self," which they called vainglory.[5]

Vainglory permeates each of the deadly sins, which manifest as particular forms of idolatry. In table 6.1, note how the seven deadly sins are listed by name, along with their particular objects of false worship. The problem is not in the objects themselves but in the place these objects occupy in our lives when we rely on them rather than God. Whenever any of these "good things" becomes a replacement for our relationship with God, it becomes a vice in our lives.[6]

Because of original sin, we are prone to all seven of these deadly sins. But in our lives we typically "specialize" in one or two capital sins, which underlie those apples we repeatedly bring to God in confession.

Table 6.1. Seven deadly sins and idolatry

DEADLY SIN	OBJECT OF IDOLATRY
Pride	Self/Accomplishments
Envy	Status/Possessions/Talents
Gluttony	Food/Drink/Drugs
Lust	Sex/Relationships/Beauty
Anger	Power/Control/Justice
Greed	Wealth/Security
Sloth	Comfort/Ease

Though I recognize all the deadly sins in my life, pride is the one I have battled with the most. Pride is inherent in our fallen nature but manifests itself uniquely in each of our lives as "an excessive belief in one's abilities that interferes with the recognition of the grace of God."[7] Pride undergirded my blasphemous thoughts and has motivated me in many ways throughout my life. I first became aware of it in my teenage years, after Dad left and I began to hide my brokenness behind various accomplishments. My pride may have looked like an abundance of self-confidence but it actually served as a remedy for my pervasive self-doubt. It became a way of hiding my feelings of shame and inadequacy. The more inadequate I felt, the more I compensated by elevating myself and idolizing myself in my accomplishments.

Each of the deadly sins hides deeper insecurities in each of our lives. Are you aware of what you are hiding through your specific deadly sins? If you use anger to gain power and control, my guess is that you struggle with feelings of powerlessness and fear. If your capital sin is greed, I would venture a guess that you have a lot of insecurity and use wealth as a way of bolstering your security and self-worth. If lust is the issue you struggle with most, I imagine that you use sex or sexual imagery to soothe the pain of rejection or feelings of not being desirable. If gluttony is your sin of choice, experience tells me that you use food, drink, or drugs to numb your pain and to fill the emptiness of abandonment in your life. If you wrestle with sloth, you have probably given up trying because it is too hard to meet others' expectations. If it is envy that consumes you, I suggest you ask yourself if you have a deep insecurity about your sense of worthiness. Are you beset by shame? Rather than face those issues in your heart, you may tear down others who have status or possessions, as did Cain with Abel (Gn 4). In each of these situations, deadly sins give the illusion of satisfying unmet needs, but in actuality they only block us from God's grace.

Are you aware of what you are hiding through your specific deadly sins?

TAKE A MOMENT

Take a moment to reflect on the deadly sins in your life and the insecurities they may be covering.

- Can you identify the specific deadly sin(s) that are most visible in your life?

- What are the objects of your idolatry behind these sins?

- What insecurities are you hiding underneath these sins and idolatries?

Since becoming aware of my pride, I have been struggling against its fierce hold for most of my adult life. Early on, I naïvely thought I could overcome it in one session of spiritual direction. With that in mind, I scheduled a session with Sister Emily, a religious sister from Wisconsin. Because she was recommended to me by my friends Jim and Lois, I went in with an open heart and a trusting disposition.

As soon as I sat down, Sister Emily asked what I wanted to focus on. "Pride," I responded. She queried, "Tell me about it." Having already prepared, I answered quickly: "For as far back as I can remember, I have been struggling with this sin of pride, and no matter how hard I try, I can't seem to get rid of it." At that, she started smiling and almost burst out in laughter. Thinking she was laughing at me, I became defensive. I thought to myself, "Here I am pouring my heart out and you are thinking it is funny. This is dead serious." I have come to realize that one of the symptoms of my pride is taking myself too seriously. Sister Emily was not being cruel or insensitive but instead was teaching me to learn to laugh at myself. She countered, "Trying to get rid of your pride is just more pride." Now I was really troubled and responded with exasperation, "See, I told you I can't seem to get rid of it." She smiled again. This time I saw her genuine compassion and kindness as she said, "You can't solve pride on your own. You have to offer it to God. He is the only one who can get rid of it." "Oh," I sighed. "That sounds too easy." Sister Emily reminded me of the scripture where Jesus said, "Come to me all you who labor and are burdened, and I will give you rest. . . . Learn from me, for I am meek and humble of heart" (Mt 11:28–29).

My time with Sister Emily taught me an important lesson: we cannot overcome the deadly sins easily or on our own. They need to be brought continually into the light through encounters with Jesus. Self-reliance will never heal us, since it is the foundation for the tree of knowledge of good and evil, the very source of our brokenness and sin.

Sometimes these deadly sins remain hidden in our lives, manifesting in the most unusual ways. Such was the case with Ana, a sweet young teenage girl whom I prayed with on my final night in Brazil, along with her friends and family. Looking at Ana, you would never guess that the deadly sin of anger was crippling her—literally and figuratively.

I discovered, through my interpreter, that Ana's right hip and foot had been injured from a car accident when she was six years old. Due to the injury to her hip, Ana's right leg was about eight inches shorter than her left. She employed a crutch that kept her from having to use her damaged right leg.

Having witnessed many miracles of healing that night, we all prayed with fervent faith and great hope. For the first ten minutes, we saw nothing that would indicate a progression of healing. Troubled by this lack of movement, I stopped and silently asked the Holy Spirit to reveal any hindrances that might be interfering with Ana's healing. Immediately, I heard the still small voice of the Holy Spirit in my thoughts: *un-forgiveness.*

When I asked Ana if she had forgiven the man who hit her with the car, tears streamed down her cheeks. She shook her head and then spoke some words in Portuguese that I did not understand. The interpreter simply translated: "She said no, she can't forgive him, because it would hurt too much."

I was amazed at this young girl's insight, recognizing that she was holding onto bitterness to protect her from suffering her deeper pain. With that confirmation, I grew even more hopeful that we would see a miraculous healing. Through my interpreter, I encouraged Ana: "I believe your leg will be healed if you forgive this man." Then I added, "Jesus will take away your pain too." This bold step of faith could have been presumptuous, but I felt unusually confident in God in that moment, as supernatural gifts of wisdom and faith were flowing freely from the Holy Spirit (1 Cor 12:8–9). While the interpreter was translating what I said, I was holding Ana's right ankle in my left hand. As soon as Ana pronounced the words of forgiveness, I felt her leg release the full eight inches in my hand, reaching normal length.

We were all amazed and began spontaneously praising Jesus for healing her. Ana was especially relieved and amazed, realizing her emotional pain had also been released. Ana's physical wound was obvious, but her deeper emotional wounds were not—neither was her "sin." Is it even fair to call her un-forgiveness a sin? As a young child, she did the only thing she knew to protect herself from the pain and traumas that overwhelmed her. My concern here is not with her moral culpability, because I believe she had very little, if any. But the decisions of her young heart had real consequences. Whether or not she chose in ignorance, she now had the choice and ability to forgive. She just needed reassurance that Jesus would be close to her as he promised. She was clearly one who fit the description of "the brokenhearted [and] those whose spirit is crushed" whom the Lord promises to be near (Ps 34:19).

All sin separates us from God in one way or another (Is 50:2). The separation can be partial or complete, depending on the gravity of our sin (*CCC*, 1854–58). At a critical moment in her young life, Ana turned a part of her heart away from God, cutting her off from experiencing his love. Whether we consider it sin or not, Ana's choice certainly became the breeding ground for later difficulties in her life just as it had for the three people suffering from depression that I mentioned in the last chapter. Like the others, Ana had been baptized and knew at some level that the Father delighted in her. She exhibited a genuine love for God and a desire to do his will. But in these certain places of her mind and heart, she had adopted self-sufficient mechanisms to protect herself from the pain of her traumas.

These self-protective and self-reliant strategies eventually become what St. Paul referred to as "fortresses" (2 Cor 10:4). Fortresses are spiritual and psychological strongholds, built invisibly in our minds and hearts, protecting us from harm. In biblical times, the meaning was much easier to grasp. Cities had walls protecting the people from invaders. These "fortresses" protected the people from harm. Drawing on that imagery, King David praised the Lord for his protection: "LORD, my rock, my fortress, my deliverer, My God, my rock of refuge, my shield, my saving horn, my stronghold!" (Ps 18:3).

King David experienced firsthand God's protection while he was being pursued by Saul's men. He could sing this psalm from the depths of his heart, because he trusted God to be his strength and protection. The Father is also our protector, our rock, and the firm foundation in our lives. But as children and teenagers many of us did not know how to turn to him in the midst of our traumas, especially when those we trusted to protect us were the ones causing us harm. Starting at a young age, we instinctively pulled our hearts away from God, especially when threatened by traumas. We turned our gaze inward toward ourselves rather than looking outward toward the Father. Wrongly thinking we were protecting ourselves, we were actually opening the doorways in our soul to demons, which were ready and waiting to establish their false protection and comfort at those times.[8]

Starting at a young age, we instinctively pulled our hearts away from God, especially when threatened by traumas.

Strongholds begin as beliefs, rooted in our minds and hearts. They are based on Satan's lies and deception. They often develop in response to traumatic wounds that have been left unhealed. It all takes place subtly and without fanfare: "A lie is planted and believed. A temptation is acted out. A wound is incurred and left to fester."[9] When these wounds are left untended, they eventually become infected by sin. Before we know it, we have been brought into spiritual slavery in a particular area of our lives.

These strongholds create barriers in our minds and hearts, which can prevent us from receiving God's love and grace and from knowing our identity as his beloved sons and daughters. Whether we are aware or not, we participate in creating these fortresses for self-protection and false comfort.[10] Think of Ana's situation. She developed a stronghold of un-forgiveness in her mind and heart to protect her from all the pain of the accident. While she received some comfort from this self-protection, it also served an unintentional function: preventing her from receiving the healing graces she so desperately desired. It also kept her heart from being open to love and intimacy. She could not get free until she invited a stronger authority—Jesus—to overcome the demonic strongman (Lk 11:14–23).

In the fourth chapter of his letter to the Ephesians, St. Paul shows how strongholds develop. They start small with our human reactions to hurt and then become doorways for demons to establish what Paul refers to as "footholds." Picture a foothold this way: Imagine a robber comes to your house and knocks on the door. Before realizing it, you open the door slightly to see who is there. Before you can stop him, the robber sticks his foot in the door, keeping it open. With his foot in the door, the robber has established a foothold. Either he will be pushed out and the door closed, or he will gain entrance, tie you up, and ransack the house. The image of being tied up is akin to what happens when the foothold becomes a stronghold. We become bound in whatever area we have allowed a foothold to grow stronger than our will to do God's will.

Paul uses the example of anger to demonstrate how we become bound by a deadly sin. He warns, "Be angry but do not sin; do not let the sun set on your anger, and do not leave room for the devil" (Eph

4:26–27). Other translations say, "Do not give the devil a foothold." He goes on to describe the bad fruit that develops when we allow the devil a foothold, including "bitterness, fury, anger, shouting, and reviling" (Eph 4:31).

We all know how these demonic expressions of anger can become footholds and strongholds in our lives. What begins as a healthy emotion signaling an injustice, if not submitted to the Holy Spirit, can become a destructive force in our lives, damaging ourselves and our relationships. What we thought was protecting us from harm actually becomes a greater source of harm, imprisoning us and hurting others. We become, as St. Paul aptly describes, slaves of our sin. We end up doing not what we want to do but rather what we hate (Rom 7:14–15). Can you relate to this in any area of your life? In any place in your life where you have felt stuck and hopeless, there is a good chance that a stronghold is in place.

I encourage you to spend considerable amounts of time journaling on these issues. With the aid of the Holy Spirit, these areas of your life can be identified and eventually healed.

Figure 6.2 on page 103 illustrates a particular expression of the tree of knowledge where anger is the stronghold. Think of the different manifestations at the top right and left of the tree as different kinds of "apples" that wound us, and those around us.

Notice the tree is rooted in ungodly self-reliance, mirroring Adam and Eve's original sin, which came about when they disobeyed God and ate the forbidden fruit from the tree of knowledge of good and evil (Gn 3:1–11). In this case, anger is the deadly sin at the trunk of the tree. The fruit on the tree reveals different ways anger can manifest in our lives. On the right side at the top of the tree are the more obvious expressions of anger such as rage, malice, slander, gossip, and so on. When these escalate we may see their extreme expressions in violence, abuse, revenge, and murder. We all know how destructive all these manifestations of anger can be. Just turn on the television and watch the daily news or practically any movie. Scripture offers many warnings for us to overcome these, with the help of God's grace.

Figure 6.2. Tree of knowledge of good and evil: anger

EXPRESSED ANGER:
Verbal abuse, insults, slander, rage, revenge, retaliation, murder, violence, malice, gossip

HIDDEN ANGER:
Self-righteousness, judgment, bitterness, resentment, depression, suicide, sickness, disease

DEADLY SIN:
Anger

ROOT OF SIN:
Ungodly Self-reliance

Each of the deadly sins has a similar root and fruit structure.

On the left side of the tree, the "apples" represent hidden symptoms of anger resulting from suppressed anger. This hidden anger can manifest as self-righteousness, judgment, depression, and physical ailments.[11] Each has a deadly consequence in our lives. Self-righteousness can keep us from seeing our need for God and blocking our ability to seek and receive his mercy. It may also mark us with an attitude of superiority, which makes us look down on others with contempt, creating isolation and broken relationships. Depression can lead us into self-hatred, in extreme cases resulting in suicide. Depression and bitterness can also bring about various kinds of physical illnesses. Research has shown that many forms of cancer, arthritis, digestive ailments, heart problems, immune system diseases, and many other physical illnesses are rooted in unresolved anger and related distresses.[12]

Can you see why anger is considered one of the seven deadly sins? Unabated in our souls it becomes lethal to ourselves and to others, creating a root of bitterness that defiles many (Heb 12:15). As a healthy emotion, anger is signaling that we or someone else has been deprived of love or has been treated unjustly. But the deadly sin of anger takes what is healthy and life giving and turns it into something destructive. Unaddressed, this deadly anger can become life-threatening at many levels. It kills our bodies by disease, our souls by restricting our capacity to love, and our spirits by cutting us off from an intimate relationship with God. It also interferes with our most intimate relationships. That is what happened to Ana, as well as John, the young man whose

As a healthy emotion, anger is signaling that we or someone else has been deprived of love or has been treated unjustly.

amazing story we will address in the next chapter, "Anatomy of a Wound."

TAKE A MOMENT

Before we turn our attention to the next chapter, I want to encourage you to spend time in prayer and self-reflection, examining your own personal tree with a specific deadly sin at its base.

- What are the "apples" that you keep facing over and over in your life?

- Draw the tree that produces these apples. Make sure to start at the roots (ungodly self-reliance), then identify the trunk (specific deadly sin), and finish by identifying the fruit that this deadly sin produces in your life (e.g., the apples).

95% illness is from anxiety

*Secant   Gnawled
   ↓   lose
Maturity   Grow in
   ↓   lose
Ronb   Read
             Frus   Time*

CHAPTER SEVEN

ANATOMY OF A WOUND

*Shame . . . seems to shake the very foundation of [our]
existence. A certain fear is always part of the very essence
of shame.*

Pope John Paul II,
Man and Woman He Created Them

At the end of the last chapter, I mentioned a young man named John.
You would like John if you met him. A popular leader in a campus
ministry, he won the admiration of his peers with his ardent zeal and
infectious joy. The first day I met him, I was drawn to his enthusiasm and genuine love for Jesus. From all external appearances John
seemed as if he had it all together, but inwardly he struggled with
an underlying sense of shame. Like Ana, a deep root of bitterness
had formed in his heart at a very young age. He was two years old
when his heart closed off to love. By the time he was twelve, he was
addicted to alcohol, drugs, and pornography.

John was twenty-one when I met him, and by then, he had already received considerable freedom and healing, beginning with an
Alcoholics Anonymous program and culminating with a powerful
retreat experience with a local campus ministry. Leaving the retreat,
John felt confident that he had indeed been delivered from his addic-
tive habits. He never felt better in his life.

For the next several weeks, John experienced the unparalleled high of the Holy Spirit. Drugs and alcohol never even crossed his mind, except as a subject of thanksgiving to God for his deliverance. But coming down from his spiritual high a few weeks later, John was thrown completely off balance. In the absence of cocaine and alcohol, his sexual addiction from years before came raging to the surface, bringing intense shame and a feeling of being completely out of control. In the months to follow, he lived in fear of being exposed. Not knowing what else to do, he wisely went to his pastor, confessed his sin, and attempted to start over. But then John failed again . . . and again . . . and again, week after week, month after month. Seeing his earnest desire and ever-deepening self-loathing, John's pastor generously promised to help him through his struggle, providing bimonthly spiritual direction, encouraging him to continue attending daily Mass, and offering confession whenever John needed it. This spiritual medicine, from the tree of life, helped John tremendously, but his sexual compulsions kept him eating the fruit from the tree of knowledge of good and evil.

Even with the extra abundance of graces from spiritual direction and the sacraments, which bore fruit in many ways, John kept worshipping the god of sex, expressed in the unholy trio of pornography, fantasy, and masturbation. No matter how hard he tried, he could not resist temptation for more than three weeks at a time. He seemed to have little or no willpower to resist the seductive power of lust. Applauding John's effort but realizing something more was needed, the pastor referred John to me for therapy. I met with John for several sessions of counseling, offering the best professional help I knew how to give. He followed all my recommendations and honestly expressed his struggles. But despite both of our best efforts, we saw little progress. No matter what John tried, he kept falling back into his sexual compulsions. Finally, realizing we were confronting a demonic stronghold, I proposed to John that both of us fast and pray between meetings. I pointed out to him that Jesus taught his disciples to do this to help another young man find freedom (Mk 9:29).

At our next session, we discovered that we had received the same direction from the Holy Spirit in our time of prayer and fasting—to bring every thought and imagination into the light of Christ (see 2 Cor 10:5). John's answer came through a book by Patrick Carnes, one of the pioneers in the field of sexual addiction, instructing John to face his fantasies and bring them out into the open.[1] In my prayer time, I was reminded of another man who had gained freedom from a sexual compulsion, by exposing his dark fantasies and shame to Jesus through prayer. I received the added insight that John's fantasies, though unholy, concealed legitimate unmet needs and good desires that were driving his sexual compulsions.

Our direction from the Holy Spirit was clear, but neither of us seemed particularly happy about following his guidance. John was afraid of exposing these secret fantasies. Entering into them meant walking headlong into his deepest shame.[2] For me as a therapist, exploring these intimate and erotic images in John's mind felt like a violation of his privacy. I also didn't want either of us to be aroused in any way by him reliving the fantasy. But because we were both convinced that this was God's idea and not ours, we reluctantly obeyed.

I will spare the details, except for one important piece of information. Part of John's fantasy was focused on a woman's breast. This is important for you to know, because the rest of what happened wouldn't make sense without that fact. As soon as John began to describe this part of his fantasy, I sensed the Holy Spirit nudging me to stop and invite him to enter into a prayer of the heart. I waited, wanting to make sure it was the Holy Spirit and not my discomfort. After a few seconds of silent prayer, I realized this was exactly what was needed. John's response immediately confirmed my prompting. After a few minutes of silence and listening prayer, John began to sob uncontrollably, signaling we were indeed touching deep repressed pain from a root memory. I sat quietly with him, feeling the

Father's love and compassion and giving him the room to feel his inner anguish.

When he was finally able to speak, John shared with me the images he saw in prayer. The first involved a memory of himself at two years old watching his mother breastfeed his baby sister. As he shared what he saw in his imagination, he began to cry again. Do you wonder how *that* memory could cause so much pain? Me too! I was astonished that such a pure and innocent image could not only cause his pain but also be a driving force behind his sexual impurity and shame. Still strongly sensing the presence of the Holy Spirit, I trusted we were moving in the right direction, but I remained bewildered as to what he was showing us. I could see that John was experiencing the searing pain of abandonment, but nothing in the image gave me a clue regarding its source.

Over the next fifteen minutes, the picture became clearer. John explained, "That is the first time I remembered that experience, but I know it is real. It makes sense of everything." I was glad it did for him, because I was still bewildered. With his new understanding, John continued, "I was envious of my sister, because she had what I wanted, my mother's love and nurturance. I resented my sister and hated my mother. I swore to myself, 'I will never need anything from my mother again.' And from then on, my heart has been shut off from my mother's love. I have looked for any way I can to satisfy that unmet need. I now understand why I am always fantasizing about women's breasts. I need nurturance and connection."

As John shared his insights from the Holy Spirit, he began to cry again, allowing me to trust that even if I didn't fully understand, it was all real to him. Still not sure what was causing his hatred for his mother and sister I continued to pray, asking Jesus to show us anything he wanted John to know. A few minutes later, John was beaming with joy and shared with me the second image the Holy Spirit had revealed to him in prayer: "Jesus came over to me as a two-year-old and picked me up. Immediately, I felt calm and loved. Then Jesus brought me over to *his* mother, letting me know that he was sharing her with me. As the Blessed Mother held me and nursed me, I felt deeply nurtured and protected."

As John spoke, I sensed the goodness of what he was sharing but wondered about the authenticity of this imagery. Was this another fantasy, or was this really the Holy Spirit guiding his imagination? All I knew was that we had prayed, asking Jesus to show him something, and he now had the fruit of the Spirit (love, joy, and peace) present where it had not been a few minutes before. Jesus said we would know by the fruit (Mt 7:16). The initial fruit was good, but it was way too early to examine the long-term fruit. As I was wondering about all this, I thought of another John (the Beloved), who, in the midst of great anguish at the foot of the cross, had also received the gift of Jesus' mother: "Woman, behold, your son. . . . [Son,] behold, your mother" (Jn 19:26b–27a). Was this what was going on? Was this John sitting in front of me receiving Mary as his mother? What about the nursing part? Was that pure? Was it from God? How could it be real when it was all in his imagination? I didn't want to squelch the Holy Spirit or ruin John's joy, so I decided I would test it all by the long-term fruit.

When John came back the next time, he seemed like a different person. He had a newfound hope and joy and was filled with gratitude for what Jesus had done for him. He told me that a few days after our meeting, when he received the Sacrament of Reconciliation, he finally could believe that he was forgiven by Jesus. Until his healing experience, John's shame had kept him from receiving the abundant grace inherent in the sacrament. On the surface it certainly seemed that all the fruit was good. John was free from his sexual compulsion for several months following, and then he graduated and moved out of town. What I didn't know is that John still harbored un-forgiveness toward his mother and sister. I would find out later that God had revealed another memory that he did not share with me, because he was not ready to face these deeper wounds. These turned out to be crucial pieces to the puzzle of his healing process. It would be another ten years before I heard the rest of the story, which I will share with you later in this book.

As John's story illustrates, our *responses* to the wounds we experience often have more of a long-term impact on us than the traumas themselves. The traumas can be horrific or relatively minor, but our responses determine whether or not we allow strongholds to develop. The reasons John felt abandoned and rejected by his mother were still largely hidden from our view, but his responses to the trauma were readily apparent. During our prayer time together, the Holy Spirit revealed these responses: John internalized the belief that he was alone and unloved. He judged his mother as unloving, and his response was to reject her love entirely. Separating his heart from hers, he felt even more alone and unlovable. He also envied his sister for having what he didn't: his mother's nurturance. On top of that, he made a vow to himself that he would never need anything from his mother again. Even though he was only two years old, these decisions, made by his own free will, had a lasting impact. John's responses to hurt opened the door to the deadly sins of anger (hatred toward his mother), envy (resentment toward his sister), lust (pornography, masturbation, and fantasy), and pride (judgments and self-sufficiency).

John's response is not different from many of our responses when wounded. Whether conscious or not, our response to the inevitable wounds in life come from one of the two trees. When we respond "in the Spirit" (tree of life), by facing our pain in communion with Jesus, we grow in security, maturity, and purity. Conversely, when we respond "in the flesh" (tree of knowledge), these traumatic wounds can plague us for the rest of our life, until they are healed. Given our spiritual weaknesses (concupiscence), the "flesh" response comes more easily.

Figure 7.1 illustrates the process of how these strongholds are formed. Each of the three concentric circles represents a different aspect of our

response to trauma. Looking at the circles from inside out, we have our wounds, our beliefs, and then our vows. Together they form a fortress of self-protection (a stronghold), representing layers of insulation around our heart, a futile attempt at protecting us from further pain.

Figure 7.1. Anatomy of a wound

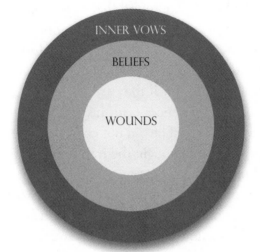

Notice that the inner circle is titled "wounds." This represents the traumatic events that cause injury to our body, soul, and spirit. According to the Life Model, developed by a team of psychologists and neurologists, wounds can occur in one of two general ways: either through the deprivation of love (type A traumas) or through unloving actions that violate our personal boundaries in some way (type B traumas). Type A traumas are most common but can be easily overlooked. These may include "not being cherished and celebrated by one's parents; not knowing we are a delight; not being understood or nurtured; not receiving appropriate discipline or boundaries; not being able to develop personal freedom or talents."[3] Have you ever thought of these as wounds or traumas?

Type B traumas, on the other hand, are the bad things that happen to us. They are what we typically think of as traumatic events:

death, divorce, violence, verbal abuse, sexual abuse, abandonment by a parent or spouse, witnessing someone else being abused or injured, and so forth.[4]

Both types of trauma inflict pain and suffering, which then become permanently stored in our brains and in every cell of our bodies. That is the conclusion of Wilder Penfield, a neurosurgeon at McGill University in Montreal, who made his discoveries while doing surgery on the brain.[5] He found that our brain records all of our experiences. When probed, our brain remembers every perception and feeling associated with those experiences. Even when not conscious, these memories influence our thoughts, actions, and behavior for the rest of our life, until they are healed.

John's traumatic experiences with his mother were stored in his mind, body, and spirit even if he did not consciously remember. When we prayed, the Holy Spirit brought them to the surface. John's wounds appeared to be from some kind of type A trauma, due to the deprivation of the nurturance he needed. In the prayer image where John's mother was breastfeeding his sister, neither was obviously doing anything to hurt John. But John's pain told me that there was indeed another more severe trauma that he had experienced. I later discovered that John had experienced a type B trauma prior to the memory he shared with me.

When traumas are left untended they create wounds in our souls that can eventually harm our bodies and spirits in significant ways. These wounds become part of our everyday language and reveal the effects of sin in our lives. We speak freely about feeling rejected, confused, abandoned, afraid, and so forth. Each of these wounds is a particular taste of hell, bringing torment to our soul. To my knowledge, though these wounds fill the pages of scripture and Christian literature, we have nothing formalized in the Church specifically cataloging our wounds. For that reason, I have drawn from the work of Ed Smith, a therapist and ordained minister, who developed Theophostic Prayer

Ministry. After years of observing the areas where people ⸺
Ed identified eight common ways we are wounded.[6] I foun
to be consistent with my own personal and professional exp
Fitting with our rich Catholic tradition, I have reduced his list by one
(by including "tarnished" in the term "shame"). From here on out I
will refer to them as the seven deadly wounds.[7]

As we will discover in the next chapter on redemptive suffering,
Jesus bore these seven wounds on the cross at Calvary. We often
talk about his physical wounds, but I believe his seven soul wounds
caused him the greatest anguish.

Table 7.1 lists the seven deadly wounds, with the accompanying
identity beliefs associated with them.

Table 7.1. Seven deadly wounds and associated beliefs

SEVEN DEADLY WOUNDS	IDENTITY BELIEFS
Abandonment	I am all alone; no one cares or understands.
Fear	I am afraid; if I trust I will be hurt/die.
Powerlessness	I can't change it; I am too small/weak.
Hopelessness	Things will never get better; I want to die.
Confusion	I don't understand what is happening.
Rejection	I am not loved, wanted, or desired.
Shame (Tainted)	I am bad, dirty, shameful, stupid, and worthless. (Because of what happened to me I am unlovable; I will never recover.)

Notice that each of the seven deadly wounds has a corresponding
identity belief. When we are wounded, we often internalize messages
about ourselves. This in turn deeply affects our identity, the way we
see ourselves. We may believe with our intellects that we are God's
beloved children, but our hearts believe a different message. For example, when we are rejected, we may believe we are not wanted,

ʋved, or desired. When we experience shame, we may internalize the belief that we are bad, dirty, worthless, stupid, and so forth.

✧

In our circle (figure 7.1), you may remember that beliefs make up the middle circle, representing how identity lies and judgments are used to insulate us from the impact of the traumas. Initially our distorted beliefs protect us from feeling pain, but in the long-term they become part of the mechanism by which our pain gets locked into our body and soul. These distorted beliefs become the building blocks that form the strongholds in our minds and hearts. Beliefs about our identity, such as the ones listed in table 7.1, shape the way we see ourselves and become filters through which we view life in all its many aspects. For John, some of those beliefs were as follows: I am alone and unlovable. My sister gets all the love. My mother doesn't love me. My father ignores me. God abandoned me too. As you can see, John's beliefs extend beyond his own identity and color his perception of his mother and father, his sister, and even God. These judgments can bind us throughout our lives.

Initially our distorted beliefs protect us from feeling pain, but in the long-term they become part of the mechanism by which our pain gets locked into our body and soul.

Scripture warns that our ungodly judgments do damage to our own souls (Rom 2:1–3; Lk 6:37–42). God's wisdom reveals that when we judge others we condemn ourselves and that the measure we use with others will be measured back to us. In other words, the judgments we hold cut off our hearts from the people whose love we need, all the while increasing our personal sense of shame and self-condemnation. John's self-condemnation (I am not lovable) increased as he grew older. This became the source of his paralyzing shame, which fueled his addictions.

Remember how God taught me about my judgments (in chapter 2) with the movie *Good Will Hunting* and through the blasphemy I uttered in my heart, *What in the hell is so good about God?* These judgments toward God, as well as Margie, Dave, and Dad, were formed from beliefs that surrounded my early traumas. They were the way I protected myself from the pain of rejection and abandonment. In addition to these judgments, I formed corollary beliefs about myself, believing I was alone and unlovable and not worth my dad's sacrifice. Can you see how all of this deeply shaped my identity and my relationships with God and others?

These beliefs became strongholds, eventually "raising [themselves] against the knowledge of God" (2 Cor 10:5). In other words, these beliefs were not in keeping with God's truth but came from the "father of lies" (Jn 8:44). Though they seemed true to me, they were actually false, intended to keep me from trusting God and receiving his love. These lies became fortresses of self-protection, guarding my heart from feeling the pain and from being hurt again.

In a similar way, John formed beliefs about his mother, women, intimacy, God, and himself as a way of guarding against the pain of abandonment and rejection. By cutting himself off from his mother, he ensured that he would stay stuck in the wound of abandonment. By rejecting and judging his mother, he kept his heart bound in the very rejection he was trying to avoid. His judgments covered his deep sense of shame that believed, "I am unlovable. I must not be worth loving and being nurtured." In response to his wounds of powerlessness and confusion, John also made inner vows, providing him an illusion of control. In reality, these vows ended up pushing him to be out of control with his addictions.

Inner vows, represented by the outermost circle in figure 7.1, are decisions we make consciously or unconsciously to protect ourselves, comfort ourselves, and take care of ourselves, usually in the midst of chaos and trauma. At times of feeling out of control, we gain a false sense of security and control in the face of pain. These vows also serve as barriers around our hearts in many ways. Perhaps this is why Jesus was so stern in warning us not to make any vows (Mt 5:33–37). We are instructed to simply submit to God's will in humility; anything else is considered prideful arrogance (Jas 4:15–17).

These unholy vows are quite different from the holy vows we pronounce as part of the sacraments. Inner vows are often taken unconsciously, in the depths of our hearts in response to fearful circumstances. In contrast, sacred vows are spoken publicly for everyone to witness. For example, our baptismal vows, which we renew every Easter in the Catholic Church, are proclaimed publically and with great humility and are witnessed by Christ and his Church. We recognize that these sacred vows are made not with human strength but with God's strength. The sacraments are the means of grace and strength in our life. They establish godly strongholds that give us security in Jesus, mature us in Christ-like virtue, and ultimately bring purity of heart. These vows flow from the tree of life.

> *The sacraments are the means of grace and strength in our life. They establish godly strongholds that give us security in Jesus, mature us in Christ-like virtue, and ultimately bring purity of heart.*

Conversely, our ungodly inner vows originate in the tree of knowledge and are born from pride. They separate us from our communion with Jesus and deny God's grace, repeating the Pelagian heresy condemned in the fourth century that proposed we could be good without God (i.e., ungodly self-reliance).[8] Jesus told us that apart from him we can do nothing (Jn 15:6). Our fallen nature desires to do everything apart from God. This is what the original sin is all about. The tree of knowledge of good and evil is rooted in the belief that we can live life our way, on our own terms. And yet that is exactly the pattern an ungodly inner vow establishes for our life. No matter how young or old we are, every unholy vow sets us on a path of ungodly self-sufficiency, where we attempt to be our own god rather than trusting God.

❧

I personally came to the realization of the difference between a God-inspired vow and an ungodly vow during my thirties, during a time when Margie and I reached a crisis point in our marriage. Our marriage vows, made in the grace of the Sacrament of Matrimony, kept us together. My inner vows, formed in my heart when I was a teenager, almost led me to follow the same path as my parents in divorce, the very thing I had judged and wanted to prevent. Our marital crisis came when I turned thirty-three years old, the exact age Dad was when he left home. After he left, I remember lying in bed at night feeling very alone, unprotected, and afraid. I did not have the language then, but huge and gaping wounds of abandonment, rejection, and fear had settled into my soul. After Dad left, we did not hear from him for nearly two years. I thought he had died. My thirteen-year-old logic reasoned, *Dad is the same age as Jesus (thirty-three) when he died on the cross, so Dad must be dead.*

I could only tolerate living in this fearful place for so long. After a while, I began to insulate myself, unconsciously forming judgments toward my dad. Without realizing it, I coupled these judgments with corresponding inner vows. *I will not be unfaithful, like my dad. I will never leave my wife and children. I will never divorce. I will never let drinking control my life.* I also added some judgments and vows for my mom: *I will never be needy like my mom. I will not let anyone hurt me like Dad hurt Mom.*

You may think these are good vows. I thought so too, but many years later I had a rude awakening. As much as these vows may have looked like my sacred marriage vows, they were worlds apart. My marriage vows were positive, focused on loving Margie faithfully in communion with Jesus. My ungodly inner vows were made in fear, judgment, and pride. They kept me from seeing Margie clearly for many years. I was living instead in the shadow of my broken child-hood and wounds from my family of origin. I was bound by these vows. They were shackles around my heart and around our mar-riage, choking the life out of our love. Rather than prevent me from repeating my parent's path, they led me right into it.

The same thing happened with the young man John. His vow "to never need anything from his mother" ended up setting him on a path of self-destruction, actually cutting off his heart from his source of nurturance and love. This area of his heart was formed in pride and resisted God's grace, just as my wounds, vows, and beliefs kept my heart walled off from God's love and healing power.

John and I had very different experiences, but we both ended up responding to trauma in ways that kept us bound for decades. Wheth-er we consider these responses "sins" or not, we can see how they gave room to the seven deadly sins we discussed in the last chapter. These wounds, beliefs, and vows often remain underground for many years, since they make up the root system of our personal "trees."

Now, as we near the end of part two, "Facing Our Brokenness," it is time to integrate all we have learned so far. Figure 7.2 illustrates John's particular tree of knowledge of good and evil. As you exam-ine it, start from the top and proceed down to the roots.

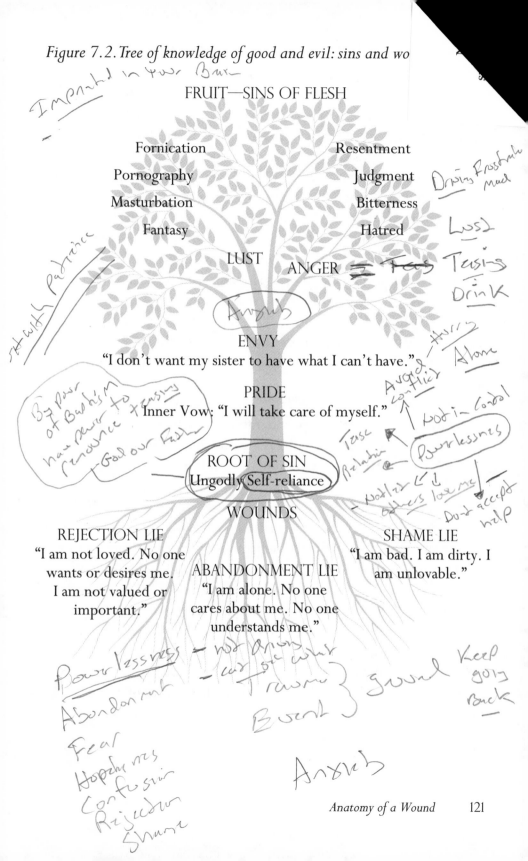

Figure 7.2. Tree of knowledge of good and evil: sins and wo

FRUIT—SINS OF FLESH

Fornication	Resentment
Pornography	Judgment
Masturbation	Bitterness
Fantasy	Hatred

LUST   ANGER

ENVY
"I don't want my sister to have what I can't have."

PRIDE
Inner Vow: "I will take care of myself."

ROOT OF SIN
Ungodly Self-reliance

WOUNDS

REJECTION LIE
"I am not loved. No one wants or desires me. I am not valued or important."

ABANDONMENT LIE
"I am alone. No one cares about me. No one understands me."

SHAME LIE
"I am bad. I am dirty. I am unlovable."

Notice John's "apples" toward the top of the tree. These are the specific sins he brought to confession. On the trunk and limbs of the tree, you see the strongholds of four of the seven deadly sins: pride, envy, anger, and lust. These produced the bad fruit in his life.

Looking down at the base of the tree, you can see how John's inner vow undergirded his prideful self-sufficiency. At the bottom, in the root system, look at how his specific wounds kept John's heart bound. Finally, see how his identity beliefs kept him from believing he was beloved by the Father and thus blocked him from receiving his healing.

As you continue to study John's personalized version of the tree of knowledge of good and evil, notice how the various strongholds are all interconnected and interdependent. John's wounds fueled his pride, which gave voice to his vows. His pride also fed his envy toward his sister. These, in turn, gave power to the strongholds of anger and lust. As you examine the trunk and the branches of this tree, notice that instead of maturing in virtue, John's tree became filled with various vices.

Pay close attention to the "fruit" of each of these deadly sins. Lust is manifested in the form of pornography, fantasy, masturbation, and fornication. Likewise John's envy toward his sister and deadly sin of anger gave strength to strongholds of bitterness, un-forgiveness, hatred, and resentment.

Rather than being securely planted in the good soil of the Father's love, John's heart remained separated by the ways he responded to his wounds. When he made the defiant decision in his heart to "never need anything from his mother," it set him up for a lifetime of vain attempts to comfort his empty heart. Though he made the vow out of a desire to protect himself from the pain, the vow actually left him unprotected. It uprooted his young heart from his mother's love and from God's. Though both still loved him, he couldn't receive it.

All of this left John feeling perpetually rejected, abandoned, and inherently unlovable (shame). Note that these wounds are listed at the bottom of the tree, underneath the ground and invisible to the natural eye.

Back in chapter 3 we invited Jesus to heal our ⟨...⟩
progressively answering our prayers. Are you beg...
bigger picture from a whole person perspective (chapter 5): ⟨...⟩
story exemplifies all of our brokenness in some way. All of us have
specific wounds and sins that contribute to our particular "apples."
John's fantasies, born from the sin of lust, had deeper roots in other
deadly sins and wounds.

Like the rest of us, John needed the good medicine of the Holy
Spirit (from the tree of life) to heal his wounds. He needed to humble himself and face his brokenness in order to receive the healing he
so deeply desired. John's story is a sobering illustration of how we
can be set up for life by the choices we make, the ravages of original
sin, and the lies of the evil one. Our particular issues may be unique,
but all of the children of Adam and Eve share this tree of knowledge
in common. This is true for all of us even after coming into the kingdom of God through baptism (CCC, 1264; Gal 5:19–22).

TAKE A MOMENT

I invite you now to fill out the bottom of your tree, which you began in the last chapter. This time, focus on the root structure of
wounds, *beliefs*, and *inner vows*.

- Can you identify the specific wounds in the roots of your tree?
  Write them down.   *No Powerlessness ⟨...⟩*

- Underneath the wounds, write out the identity beliefs associated
  with them.

- What inner vows made from those wounds undergird your
  self-sufficiency?

Trauma

Pain

Rejection

Pride Envy Lust Anger Gluttony

Self Richeus

Abandonment

1 Spiritual
2 Relational
3 Mind
4 Body
5 Shame Neuton

Now that we have faced our brokenness and come to some deeper understanding of it, we are ready to turn to part 3, "Healing Our Wounds."

PART THREE
HEALING OUR WOUNDS

Bring all you are suffering to [Jesus] . . . only open your heart to be loved by Him as you are. He will do the rest.

Blessed Mother Teresa of Calcutta,
Letter to the Missionaries of Charity Family

CHAPTER EIGHT

REDEMPTIVE SUFFERING

We must bear the victory of Christ's Cross to everyone everywhere. . . . Christ's Cross embraced with love does not lead to sadness, but to joy!

Pope Francis,
Palm Sunday, 2013

In part one of this book, we set out on a journey to encounter Jesus as the good teacher, the compassionate healer, and the beloved Son. In part two, we examined our brokenness from a whole person perspective and explored how many of our physical and psychological symptoms have their roots in the seven deadly sins and seven deadly wounds. Now in part three, we are seeking to bring this brokenness to Jesus, asking him to heal our wounds and free us from the strongholds of sin that so easily entangle us. With that purpose in mind, we will be focusing our attention on three powerful medicines from the tree of life: redemptive suffering, the sacraments, and healing prayer. As we begin this chapter on redemptive suffering, I encourage you to keep these two questions in the forefront of your mind:

- How is Jesus' redemptive suffering a means of our personal healing?
- How can our own redemptive suffering be a source of healing for ourselves and others?

The Passion and Human Suffering

In the majesty of divine providence, I am writing this chapter during Holy Week, when the entire Church pauses to contemplate in greater depth this mystery of Jesus' passion, death, and resurrection. During this most beautiful and healing season of the liturgical year, we are encouraged by Pope Francis to "bear the victory of Christ's Cross" with love and lasting joy. Many of us wonder how this is even possible as we watch the effects of evil play out daily in the world around us and experience it intimately in our own lives.

Several years ago, during Holy Week, I went with members of our parish community to see the movie *Passion of the Christ*. I knew it would not be easy to watch, but it ended up being harder than I imagined, especially during the scene of Jesus' scourging. I wanted to turn away as I saw Jesus brutalized by the soldiers' repeated lashings. With each crushing blow, as more blood oozed from his torn flesh, I numbed myself all the more. I could understand with new depth the words of Psalm 38: "I am numb and utterly crushed; I wail with anguish of heart" (Ps 38:9).

In the Garden of Gethsemane Jesus wailed as his heart was filled with anguish (Mt 26:36–38), but here at the pillar he was simply numb and utterly crushed. His mother, Mary, his followers, and all the other onlookers were similarly traumatized, as were many of us who watched the re-enactment.

Whether as observers or participants we all know soul-numbing trauma in our lives: death's anguish, the tearing apart of hearts and families through divorce, the violence of abuse; the list goes on. Suffering is all around us and has touched each of our lives personally, in one way or another. All we need to do is turn on the evening news and it is right before our eyes. And every single day we wake up in the morning to carry our own crosses, big or small.

Yet in the midst of it, we are encouraged to carry these crosses with joy and not sadness. How is this possible?

If you are anything like me, your instinct is to run from suffering and turn away from all the overwhelming pain that surrounds it. We all have a healthy repugnance for every form of evil and the suffering that accompanies it. This is natural. Our first and most natural response is to avoid it at any cost.

When we speak of redemptive suffering we are not suggesting that suffering itself is good. As Pope John Paul II affirms in his encyclical *On Human Suffering*, suffering is an experience of evil.[1] There is nothing glamorous about evil or its effects, and the Cross makes this perfectly clear for all to see. Even Jesus prayed that his cup of suffering would be taken away from him, before surrendering to his Father's will for our sakes (Mt 26:3). He knew that he was about to enter into the most difficult battle with evil that any human

Suffering is an experience of evil.

being could ever face. And yet he did it willingly, because he knew that his suffering would redeem the entire world.

If the passion story were to end with the crucifixion, we would have no choice but to resign ourselves to the inevitable despair of spending our lives in misery. This would be hell on earth. But the Gospel story does not end in meaningless suffering and despair. "In the Cross of Christ not only is the redemption accomplished through suffering, but also human suffering itself has been redeemed."[2] Jesus didn't remain stuck on the cross or in death; he triumphed in the Resurrection. As the Church proclaims with one voice at Easter: "He is Alive!" Because of Christ's victory over sin and death, the Cross has become the font of our healing and redemption.

Jesus Conquers Evil

All suffering is traumatic in some way, but not all of it is redemptive. In the last chapter we spoke about the long-lasting impact of our traumatic experiences. That impact is largely dependent on the way we respond. In Jesus, we have the exemplar for how to respond to trauma from the tree of life. Through everything he suffered he continued to rely on his Father and not on himself, and thus responded to the most horrific evil by bringing about the greatest good ever known in the history of mankind.

Take a moment and reflect with me on all that Jesus accomplished on our behalf in his redemptive suffering. We are assured in scripture that he "took away our infirmities and bore our diseases" and that "he was pierced for our offenses, crushed for our sins" (Mt 8:17; Is 53:5). But what does that really mean at a practical level in each of our lives? How may we personally appropriate the graces Jesus won for us on the Cross? These are not easy questions to answer, because they involve great mysteries, but somehow we must explore these mysteries in order for Jesus' death and resurrection to be real medicine for our bodies and souls.

How may we personally appropriate the graces Jesus won for us on the Cross?

Overcoming the Seven Deadly Sins

Most of us have at least some appreciation and understanding of the great benefits of Christ's redemptive sacrifice. In bearing the entire penalty and punishment for our sins, he made it possible for us to live without condemnation and guilt (Rom 8:1). Because "he was pierced for our offenses and crushed for our sins" (Isa 53:5) we are enabled to come before the Father without fear of rejection (Heb 4:16). No matter how terrible our offenses, we have the assurance, in Christ, that we will be completely accepted when we bring our sins out into the light and receive his forgiveness (1 Jn 1:5–10). (More on this in the next chapter with my brother Dave's story.)

But that is not all Jesus accomplished for us through his passion, death, and resurrection. Too often we stop at the fact that our sins are forgiven and we despair at ever overcoming them. We fail to realize that our deadly sins have become strongholds that will require powerful weapons for them to be overcome (2 Cor 8:4). Jesus showed us how to overcome these deadly sins by responding in the opposite spirit. Facing his suffering with the aid of the Holy Spirit, he exhibited the lively virtues in the face of every deadly sin.[3]

Table 8.1. Seven lively virtues

DEADLY SINS/VICES	LIVELY VIRTUES
Pride	Humility/Meekness
Envy	Kindness/Gratitude
Gluttony	Fasting/Moderation
Lust	Chastity/Self-Control
Anger	Longsuffering/Surrender
Greed	Generosity/Stewardship
Sloth	Diligence/Faithfulness

Let's consider how Jesus conquered the evil associated with each of these deadly sins. In confronting the *pride* of the rulers, Pharisees, and guards, Jesus responded with total *humility*. He does the same in response to our arrogance, haughtiness, and pride. As we grow in communion with him, we learn to be meek and humble of heart, as he is (Mt 11:29).

When Jesus felt the full force of their anger, hatred, and rage, he *patiently endured*, *surrendering control* and giving up his right for revenge. In the end, his only response was to forgive those who hurt him, including all of us who have been destructive with our anger. By abiding in him, we can endure our suffering patiently, rather than react in anger.

Jesus hung on the cross as a direct result of the insidious *envy* of the devil expressed through each of these leaders who were filled with raging jealousy. Bearing the wickedness that springs from our envy as well, he responds simply with *kindness* and brotherly love. His compassion and genuine concern for our well-being is a beautiful witness for all of us, teaching us to be *grateful* for what we have been given and to look out for the needs of others, even in our pain.

In response to the indifference of the bystanders and our own *sloth*, Jesus remained *diligent*, fully engaged and faithful to the end. Combating our *greed*, he *offered everything*, down to his last bit of clothing, even his very self—body and blood, soul and divinity. Through it all, he trusted completely in the Father's providence. His example teaches us to work diligently and to trust the Father in all circumstances, no matter how threatening they may seem.

Do not return evil for evil . . . but, on the contrary, a blessing, because to this you were called, that you might inherit a blessing. (1 Pt 3:9)

Overcoming our *gluttony*, he displayed the epitome of *moderation*, abstaining from any drugs or satiation on the cross, though he was emaciated and thirsty. For our *lust*, he bore the ridicule of all. Stripped naked and laid bare, he became the pure, undefiled Lamb of God and chaste bridegroom. All of our self-indulgence is exposed by him, and by his Spirit we are enabled to exercise *self-control and chastity*.

Jesus' incredible strength and love in the face of suffering is amazing, isn't it? In him, we see a man perfected in virtue. "When he was insulted, he returned no insult; when he suffered, he did not threaten" (1 Pt 2:23). While we admire him, we also have to wonder about ourselves. How in the world can we possibly emulate him? Yet this is precisely what we are called to do, with his grace, in the face of every injury in our life. "Do not return evil for evil . . . but, on the contrary, a blessing, because to this you were called, that you might inherit a blessing" (1 Pt 3:9).

Obviously we cannot do this in our own strength. That would bring us back to the tree of knowledge of good and evil, relying on ourselves rather than God. But as we allow Jesus' life to grow in us, his redemptive suffering allows us to respond in the opposite spirit as he did, replacing our deadly sins with his lively virtues.

Personally, I have a long way to go in applying this in my daily life. But I have learned to be grateful for the little and small ways that I see God's grace operating in and through me. I am discovering some of the joys of redemptive suffering. One small victory, in a very ordinary situation, serves to illustrate. Margie and I were in the midst of a conversation when she said something that offended me. I felt rejected. (This in itself was a good sign of growth that I could recognize rejection and name it.) Internally voicing my hurt to the Father, I was able to avoid reacting in a similar fashion on this occasion. Instead, I felt prompted to pray in silence.

With God's strength, I refrained from retaliating with unkind words. Though a small victory, it was only a partial one. I still didn't respond in total love but instead walked away (a less obvious form of rejecting her). As I made the seemingly long journey from our living room back to our bedroom, I was still nursing my hurt. But continuing to pray, I sensed the Holy Spirit prompting me to turn around and head back to reconcile with Margie. Protesting inwardly, I realized I was still holding on to some bitterness (the deadly sin of anger) and self-righteousness (the deadly sin of pride).

I thought to myself, *she hurt me. She needs to come apologize to me.* But then I was stopped in my tracks, as the Holy Spirit showed me that I was hiding behind a self-protective wall of pride because of my fear of being rejected again (wounds of fear and rejection). I thought I was protecting myself from rejection, but I was actually rejecting Margie instead. With this new awareness, I asked the Father to forgive me and to help me to love her. Accepting his love and strengthened by his grace, I turned around and headed back to the living room, feeling more vulnerable and less self-protective this time. As I was walking, I heard the thoughts in my mind *wash her feet*, which I took to mean that I should humble myself before Margie and serve her. Still struggling, I knew I needed to express love and kindness. When I did, Margie immediately softened, and our love was repaired very quickly.

Later that evening, I stopped and asked God to show me where these feelings of rejection were rooted in my heart. I then asked him to heal these deeper wounds in me. He brought me back to some memories earlier in our marriage and from when I was a child and teenager, where I had internalized the message *I am not loved*. I needed his love in these places of my heart to heal me.

Though just a small example, this kind of redemptive suffering is the substance of everyday life. Incidents such as this one are far from insignificant. How many of our relationships would change dramatically if we could live daily this grace of redemptive suffering that brings joy and not more heartache? I long to love in this way, don't you? I believe this is what Jesus meant when he commanded us to take up our cross and follow him (Mt 16:24). Each of these "little deaths" helps to prepare us for our final death and resurrection, the ultimate healing in Christ. Only when we choose to die to our selfish reactions in these small ways will we have the grace to make the final surrender.

TAKE A MOMENT

Take a moment now to reflect on ways you have suffered in a redemptive way, by dying to your selfish reactions and choosing to love rather than retaliate.

- Sisters attack politics - ask for love

- Recall a situation where you wanted to retaliate but instead responded in kindness or forgave the person who hurt you.

- How did you deal with your own wounded heart? Did you invite Jesus into the pain?

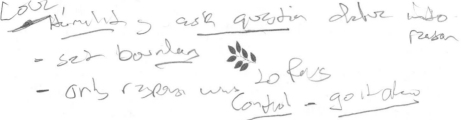

[handwritten notes: Love, Humility, ask questions, delve into person — set boundaries — only respon[d] ... to love — Control — go it alone]

Healing the Seven Deadly Wounds

Jesus never gave even the slightest foothold for the evil one through all that he suffered. He never came into agreement with the enemy's lies or gave into their power to define his identity. He refrained from any hint of bitterness, formed no ungodly judgments, and avoided self-reliant vows that might keep him from trusting completely in his Father.

Even in the midst of all the evil that threatened to overtake him, Jesus continued believing in the Father's goodness. He remained deeply rooted and grounded in the Father's love and never lost sight of his own true identity. Through his redemptive suffering, Jesus provides the supreme example for how each of us can face our own suffering with the grace of his redemptive love.

Facing the most terrifying anguish of body and soul, Jesus didn't give in to *fear* or the deceptive lies that would lead him to withhold or protect himself. Instead, he trusted his Father's protective love through every moment of his passion. Though "spurned and avoided by men" (Is 53:3) he did

> *Through his redemptive suffering, Jesus provides the supreme example for how each of us can face our own suffering with the grace of his redemptive love.*

not internalize the *shame* that invariably comes with *rejection*. Instead he "endured the cross, despising its shame" (Heb 12:2). Jesus freely chose to enter into *powerlessness* and the apparent *hopelessness* and *confusion* of the cross, but he never lost sight of God's will and mighty power. He remained anchored in the hope of the resurrection that was to come and fixed on the purposes that the Father laid out for him.

Perhaps the most painful of all was his experience of abandonment, not only from his friends and followers, but also from his ever-present Father. Who is not pierced to the core by Jesus' bellowing lament from the cross: "My God, my God, why have you forsaken me?" (Mt 27:46).

Stop and listen to Jesus utter these words from the depths of his soul. Allow his anguished cry to express your own pain of abandonment. Have you ever touched this depth of pain in your life? I have experienced it a few times in my life, most notably in facing the events of my dad leaving and in times of spiritual darkness when God seems far away. Knowing just the smallest measure of his pain, I am amazed at Jesus' confidence in the Father. Though he felt abandoned by him, he continued to turn towards him. He did not turn his back on the Father or try to take care of himself like I often do. He did not internalize the lie that he was alone or unheard. Through all his suffering, Jesus continued trusting his Father, believing he remained with him at every moment, even while the searing pain of abandonment overwhelmed all the faculties of his soul. No one cries out unless he believes someone is listening.

"My God, My God, Why Have You Abandoned Me?"

In the midst of Jesus' agony, he had the presence of mind to recite Psalm 22: "My God, my God, why have you abandoned me? Why so far from my call for help, from my cries of anguish? My God, I call by day, but you do not answer; by night, but I have no relief" (Ps

22:2–3). Do you find yourself wanting to say (or shout) the same thing at God because of events in your own life?

Most of us don't want to acknowledge these intense feelings. We fear if we do we will remain hopelessly stuck in our pain and loneliness. But the opposite is true. Denying our pain is what keeps us continuing to feel so hopelessly alone. In contrast, hope is restored when, in communion with Jesus, we face our pain and despise the shame as Jesus did in his passion and throughout his life.

TAKE A MOMENT

Take a moment and reflect on how you respond when you are deeply hurt.

- Do you face your pain with Jesus, by expressing your emotions to the Father? Or are you more likely to deny your pain and give in to identity lies?

- What do you typically do when you feel "alone and unloved"? Do you try to medicate these feelings, or do you bring them to Jesus as a way of finding communion with him?

- What kind of thoughts go through your mind when you face frightening situations in which you feel "powerless, hopeless, afraid, and confused"? Do you continue to trust the Father's providence and keep your hope fixed on him, or do you resort to vows of self-sufficiency and judge the people who are hurting you as a way of staying in control?

Pope John Paul II's Example
of Redemptive Suffering

Pope John Paul II gave the entire world a beautiful example of how to face our suffering with joy, in communion with Jesus. He knew the searing pain of abandonment, losing his beloved mother to death at the tender age of nine and his brother three years later. During his teenage years, he faced the fear of death or imprisonment almost daily and lost many friends during the war. At the age of twenty he also lost his father, after a brief illness.

Throughout his adult life he lived under the constant oppression of communism and found opposition wherever he went, responding to it all with mercy and faith, all the while proclaiming the truth first as a priest, then as a bishop, and finally as the Successor of Peter. Who can forget his kindness and compassion which he showed to the man who tried to assassinate him? Even in dying his life reflected his intimate communion with Jesus. At his funeral, one-third of the entire world looked on, because in him we all saw a genuine witness—a man who lived what he taught: "Every man has his own share in the Redemption. Each one is also called to share in that suffering through which the Redemption was accomplished. . . . Thus each man, in his suffering, can also be a sharer in the redemptive suffering of Christ."[4]

Following Jesus' example, John Paul showed the whole world how the evil of suffering can become a powerful source for good and a means of healing.

Following Jesus' example, John Paul showed the whole world how the evil of suffering can become a powerful source for good and a means of healing. He taught us that we no longer need to run in terror from the inevitable pain in our life, or resign ourselves in despair. He brought St. Paul's words to life (see Col 1:24). He rejoiced in his sufferings for the sake of the Church, continuing Christ's redemptive sacrifice in our modern world. Like St. Paul, he showed us that when we choose to participate in Jesus' redemptive suffering, we allow our worst nightmares to become rivers of healing grace for ourselves and others.

My brother Dave's story is another unforgettable example of how our worst nightmares can be transformed through redemptive suffering. Formed in the school of hard knocks during all those years on the streets as a drug addict, Dave constantly challenged my idealistic views of scripture. He challenged me to explain how Paul could find joy in suffering (cf. Col 1:24). For many years, all Dave knew was the anguish of suffering; he really didn't believe anything redemptive could come from the suffering he had experienced. None of it had brought him any closer to God. Quite to the contrary, his deadly sins and wounds became the catalyst for him running away. Even after his powerful healing through the sacraments, which I will detail in the next chapter, Dave wondered how in the world St. Paul could boast of his joy in the midst of suffering. I never made any headway in explaining it to him, probably because I lived it so poorly myself. Like most things, Dave had to find out for himself, the hard way. But once he mastered it, he became a powerful example for me and our entire family.

Soon after Dave's Christ Renews His Parish (CRHP) experience, my mom discovered she had four free airline tickets to fly anywhere in the world and had to use them before the airline went out of business. So she invited Dave, Margie, and me to accompany her on a three-week vacation to New Zealand. The entire trip turned out to be another beautiful providence from the Father. Touring the majestic countryside of New Zealand, we felt as if we were living in paradise. We relived the forgotten joy of our childhoods, jumping on trampolines, enjoying great belly laughs together, and taking in the beauty all around us. It was a glorious resurrection experience after many years of suffering as a family.

After the vacation, Dave was refreshed and decided he needed to restore his relationship with his daughter, Sarah, who was five years old at the time. Though they both tried, things didn't work out with Sarah's mother, but they agreed that Sarah could begin to live with her dad part of the time. It was indeed a new beginning and seemed almost like a fairytale ending after the difficult years of suffering and desolation. But the fairytale soon turned into a nightmare as Dave found out he was terminally ill with HIV/AIDS. In the early 1990s, AIDS was a death sentence. Dave suspected he had contracted HIV through a heroin needle, but he still held out hope that somehow it would not develop into full-blown AIDS. These hopes began to fade in the fall of 1991 as AIDS symptoms gradually began to appear in Dave's body. We were all deeply concerned, especially since he had vowed months earlier, "If I have AIDS I am going to run away where no one can find me. I would rather die alone than put everyone through that agony." We were all afraid he would go off and take enough drugs to kill himself.

Since we were spending the first Christmas at his new house, Dave decided to wait to confront his fears until after Christmas. He did not want to ruin Christmas for his daughter and everyone else. The day after Christmas, he and I sat outside on his porch alone. I could tell he wanted to tell me something and didn't want anyone else to hear. He began by telling me about his doctor's appointment the next day. "I am afraid the doctor is going to confirm my worst fear, that I do have AIDS." Before I could say anything, Dave continued, "But I have been praying about this, and I have a surprising peace inside. For a long time, I have been praying for a purpose, and I believe God is showing me this may be my answer. My purpose may be to become someone with AIDS, living for Christ." By the time Dave finished sharing, I had no words left to say. I sat there dumbfounded and in awe. I couldn't believe the spiritual maturity of my brother, who a few years earlier had been totally self-absorbed in a life of drugs and crime, and a few months earlier said he would run rather than face this with everyone. He was answering the question neither of us had been able to answer: how St. Paul could find meaning and purpose in his suffering. And sure enough, for his remaining years, Dave did just that. After confirming he had full-blown AIDS, the doctor estimated he had two years to live, assuming he took his medicine.

Watching Dave decline over the next two years was both agonizing and inspiring. Though his body was wasting away, day by day his spirit was being renewed by the Holy Spirit (2 Cor 4:16). Gradually, Dave went from a healthy 200 pounds to a frail 130 pounds, but his spirit bore the power of Christ in the midst of weakness (2 Cor 12:8–10). He became a living and dying witness of Jesus to each one of us. No one was more affected than my brother Wayne, who at the time was not practicing his faith. Wayne and Dave had always been close, and when Dave could no longer take care of himself physically, Wayne took him into his home. More than anyone else, Wayne saw the grace, joy, and love with which Dave suffered. In return, Wayne found his own heart opening as he took care of his dying brother. Dave's care eventually required us to bathe him and change his adult diapers. Wayne took the bulk of this responsibility with the help of a home health worker. The rest of us came to relieve him on the weekends. Bathing and wiping Dave was not only uncomfortable but also potentially dangerous if we did not practice good hygiene. Through all the pain and humiliation, Dave bore everything cheerfully. When any of us asked if we could help him, he would merely give a thumbs-up and say "fiat." As I am writing this, I am stunned with God's providence once again. I just realized today's date is March 25, which is the anniversary of Dave's death as well as Wayne's birthday. Nineteen years ago today, we all headed to Jacksonville to be with Dave for an early Easter and to celebrate Wayne's birthday.

Our early Easter celebration was prompted by Dad coming down from West Virginia a week early. After Mom called to let Dad know of Dave's quick decline, a friend of Dad's at work gave him a plane ticket to see his son one last time. He could not get any flights during Holy Week, so he came ten days early. We all decided to celebrate over Palm Sunday, realizing it may be our last Easter together as a whole family.

When Margie and I arrived at Wayne's home around 11:00 a.m. on Friday, March 25, no one answered the door, but we heard Dad's voice inviting us to come in. Wayne was at work, but the door was open. Not knowing what to expect, we headed back to Dave's bedroom and beheld a most troubling and glorious sight. Dave in a semi-coma, sat sprawled between my dad's legs as Dad held him from behind on the bed. Dad smiled hello, and Dave's semi-comatose stare seemed to go right through Margie and me. My heart was doubly touched by the scene. I was amazed at how the Father had orchestrated these events, once again. Seeing Dad hold Dave while he was dying was an undeniable touch of God's poetry. I was also moved to see my brother struggling to take his final breaths, knowing that he would soon be released into the arms of our heavenly Father. What a privilege to witness it all. It was pure gift from the Father, the fruit of Dave's willingness to "be someone with AIDS for Jesus." Through Dave's redemptive suffering, God was healing our family. Mom extended mercy to Dad, and Dad was again caring for the son he had abandoned. On top of that, all of us were coming together as a family, repairing on a deeper level the brokenness from divorce and Dave's drug use that had split us apart more than twenty-five years earlier.

Margie, who started her work career on a cancer floor, recognized Dave was close to death. She left the room to call everyone to tell them to come quickly. Dad got up to go to the bathroom and invited me to take his place, sliding in behind Dave, straddling him as Dad had done. I was now holding my long-lost prodigal brother, both of us reunited in the embrace of our heavenly Father, our earthly father, and each other. We had all come home. Within minutes of

Margie and Dad walking back in the room, Dave breathed his last. I felt like a midwife, assisting him in his transition from this life to the next and handing him off to the angels in heaven, who would bring him safely to the Father.

Dave had given us all a beautiful answer to the question of how to "rejoice in our suffering." My heart was full. As soon as Dave died, Dad and I embraced each other, crying and rejoicing in what we had been graced to experience. Margie, still in shock, stood back for a moment and then embraced each of us. I was crying freely in both of their arms, feeling love not only for Dave but for Dad and Margie as well. We were standing on holy ground, feeling the thick presence of the Holy Spirit in our midst.

My heart was bursting in love and gratitude to the Father. Together the three of us held hands and prayed for Dave, trusting that he would be met with a beautiful reception in heaven. We grieved as ones who have hope of the good things to come (1 Thes 4:13). As the day progressed, we were able to share the same love with each member of our family.

On the day of Dave's funeral, our immediate family stood up together as one to give his eulogy. That in itself was a source of major healing. The gospel reading, as you might guess, told the story of the prodigal son, and we all had a chance to share about Dave's journey from the pig pen back to the father's embrace. We were all celebrating together, knowing that Dave was present with us in the Communion of Saints, now wearing the white robe that Jesus purchased for him on the Cross (Rv 7:14).

TAKE A MOMENT

As you read this account of Dave's dying process, final moments, and subsequent funeral, what touches your heart?

- Is there any part of Dave's story with which you identify? In what ways? — My mom Died this way — 4-5 mo dy we took care of her God brought me home to phy dyplunch both Sconsoher Bowl , she saw smedked —

- Can you think of any circumstances in your life where intense suffering or other tragedies have been transformed into profoundly healing experiences for you, members of your family, or others?

When suffering is transformed by God's grace in this way, the events associated with it often continue to bring further healing even years later. This has been our experience with Dave's redemptive suffering. Exactly one year after his death, on March 25, several family members gathered in St. Augustine, Florida, to celebrate the first anniversary of Dave's entry into eternal life. Since it was the feast of the Annunciation of the Angel Gabriel to Mary, the priest gave a beautiful homily on Mary's fiat. He went on to say that Mary's fiat was her "yes" to everything she would experience, including Calvary, where her own heart would be pierced. In the middle of listening to the homily, we all looked at each other and smiled. Finally, we understood the meaning of Dave's thumbs up, and "fiat" in the face of all he was going through. Dave was giving his "yes" to share in Jesus' redemptive suffering. In a small way, he was following the Blessed Mother's example, as Pope John Paul II affirms: "From the time of her secret conversation with the angel, she began to see in her mission as a mother, her 'destiny' to share . . . in the very mission of her son. And she very soon received confirmation of this . . . . in the solemn words of the aged Simeon, when he spoke of a sharp sword that would pierce her heart."[5] Mary in some way represents all of us who have to accompany others we love on the path of suffering. All of our hearts are pierced when the ones we love have to undergo pain and anguish as we stand by helplessly. That was certainly true for our family, and especially our mother, as we watched Dave decline in health.

I will never forget the Good Friday that Dave and I shared two years before he died. We slowly walked the Stations of the Cross together, feeling the weight and reality of them as never before. When we arrived at the fourth station, Jesus Meets His Mother, Dave stopped and stared. I was ready to push on but soon realized he was not. Finally, he looked over at me and said, "I don't know how I am going to face Mom when I am dying." He also expressed a sense of dread at having to face my grandmother, who was like a second mom to him. Again I had no words, just tears welling up to meet the ones I noticed forming in his eyes. I finally acknowledged, "It's going to be tough." It was difficult, but we both underestimated God's grace in our weakness.

When the time finally came, Mom and Mom Margaret (our grandmother) were both prepared. Along with Wayne, they were spared from being in the room when Dave died but were not forgotten. The Father had a special gift for each of them. My grandmother said she knew immediately the moment Dave died, as she felt a presence come in the room; she recognized this as Dave's soul saying goodbye. She was deeply consoled to have her own time to say goodbye to him. My mom also said she knew immediately by another heavenly sign. She was with her brother Sam when the dark clouds that had filled the sky that day suddenly parted and a beautiful ray of sunshine appeared. At that moment she knew Dave had died. Since then, every time Mom visits Dave's gravesite, as well as on other special occasions, she says the same little miracle takes place. The dark clouds part and a burst of sun appears, and she senses Dave's smile. Now her beloved son is shining in the reflected glory of Mary's Son.

I will share more of Dave's transformation in the next chapter, as much of it came about through the sacraments.

Want to provide health, Env
— love

- Good triggers →
④
- Immediate reaction
  — thoughts
- — Actions

① Love, ② humans, ③ Ask quest

Fill softens with redemptive love
redemptive love

There is always redemption in
every tragic event

— Paralysis
— Loss of loved one
— Cancer

more compassion!

CHAPTER NINE

SACRAMENTS AND HEALING

The Church believes in Christ, the physician of souls and bodies. This presence is particularly active through the Sacraments.

Catechism of the Catholic Church, 1509

During my twenties, I remained rather indifferent to the sacraments. I could relate to Scott Hahn's comment before his deeper conversion: "Sacraments are boring."[1] Though I could recite the Baltimore Catechism with relative ease—"A sacrament is an outward sign instituted by Christ to give grace"—the words meant little to me. Like the townspeople of Nazareth whose lack of faith kept them from receiving Jesus' healing power, I lacked the faith to recognize the presence of the Divine Physician in the sacraments, and thus received little healing through them for many years.

Now I see the sacraments in a very different light. As precious gifts pouring forth from Jesus' side on the Cross, every sacrament is a tangible participation in his life, death, and resurrection (Rom 6:2–6; Eph 5:21–25). How could I have ever thought they were boring or unimportant? Quite to the contrary, I now realize the sacraments are the lifeblood of our faith, Jesus' provision for the Church's unity and healing (see 1 Cor 10–12) and the source of all goodness in society. The sacraments have existed in some form or another in all the Christian churches and throughout the entire history of the Old and New Testaments.[2]

My initial awakening to the healing power of the sacraments took place during my third Christ Renews His Parish (CRHP) weekend. If you will remember from chapter 1, I spent the first twenty-four hours of that retreat in a hellish desolation, watching everyone around me fully engage in the Spirit. Looking back I now see how an unholy spirit, which had gained entry into my mind through some occult books I had read, kept me bound in oppression. As soon as I confessed my sins and received absolution, I sensed an immediate lifting of this oppressive spirit. Soon after confession, I heard a seventeen-year-old give witness to the Real Presence of Jesus in the Eucharist. I don't remember what he said, but I remember his confident faith and joyful gratitude to Jesus. As he spoke, my spirit suddenly awakened to the Church's teaching, which I had heard about all my life but never fully believed in my heart. Like a light switch suddenly turned on, I could finally accept what I had been taught all those years.

Receiving the sacraments that night, my heart awakened from death to life. I was encountering the life-giving presence of Jesus, the physician of my soul and body. He revealed his presence in several ways: in the consecrated bread and wine; in the priest (the Sacrament of Holy Orders); and in our community united with him in the Sacraments of Baptism and Communion. We were experiencing the joy of being "one heart and mind" in our collective identity as the Body of Christ (Acts 4:32). Three hours later, as my friends and I prayed together, the graces of our Confirmations manifested in a new way, as we experienced the corporate outpouring of the Holy Spirit similar to the day of Pentecost (Acts 2:4; *CCC*, 1302). With a greater internal awareness of our baptismal identities as beloved sons, we cried out with new fervor and confidence: "Abba, Father!" (Rom 8:15).

When I returned home that weekend and embraced my wife and daughters, I felt a love I never knew before. This experience gave me a greater insight into the love Jesus called us to when we received the Sacrament of Matrimony. I caught a glimpse of what it means to love my wife (and children) "as Christ loved the church" (Eph 5:25). In less than a day, these once "boring" sacraments became alive in my heart and changed my life forever.

※

Years of reflection, aided by scripture and Church teaching, have allowed me to see how each of the sacraments played a vital role in my healing and transformation. Many teachers along the way have offered insights, including Father Raniero Cantalamessa, the respected household preacher to Pope John Paul II and Pope Benedict XVI. In his book *Sober Intoxication of the Spirit*, which I read many years after my CRHP weekend, he put words to my encounters with Jesus in the sacraments: "We can compare the sacraments to switches for electrical current" that allow the healing power of Jesus to touch each and every Christian in specific ways.[3] This was precisely my experience. I went from sensing no "electrical current" to suddenly feeling God's presence light up my soul.

But I was troubled by a nagging question. I had been receiving the sacraments for years. Why had I not experienced the healing presence of Jesus earlier? Father Cantalamessa's explanation helped me to see that the graces of my Baptism (and other sacraments) had been there all along but had not been released due to my lack of faith and the strongholds in my mind and heart:

> The outpouring of the Spirit actualizes and revives our baptism. . . . Catholic theology can help us understand

how a sacrament can be valid and legal but "unreleased" if its fruit remains bound or unused. . . . Sacraments are not magic rites that act mechanically, without people's knowledge or collaboration. . . . The fruit of the sacrament depends wholly on divine grace, however this divine grace does not act without the "yes" . . . the consent and affirmation of the person. . . . God acts like a bridegroom who does not impose his love by force, but awaits the free consent of the bride.[4]

Finally, everything was beginning to make sense. I had received God's gift of himself at my Baptism and continued to receive his healing presence through the other sacraments throughout my life. The grace had been fully given but only partially received. My lack of faith and active cooperation kept the graces largely unnoticed and bearing limited fruit in my life. Moreover, my own sins and wounds blocked God's grace from flowing freely in my life. It was as though my spiritual pipes were clogged. All those years, Jesus continued to wait patiently for my "yes" to him. He does this for each one of us. Since our free consent is essential, he waits patiently for his wounded bride, all the while wooing her until she is willing and able to receive his gift with an open heart.

Pope Francis recently reaffirmed this in a post-Easter homily: "The grace contained in the Easter sacraments is an enormous source of strength for renewal in personal and family life, as well as for social relations. Nevertheless, everything passes through the human heart . . . if I let that grace change for the better whatever is not good in me . . . then I allow the victory of Christ to affirm itself in my life. . . . This is the power of grace!—without grace we can do nothing!"[5]

TAKE A MOMENT

Notice Pope Francis's emphasis on our free will and our need for healing: "Everything passes through the human heart." The

sacraments are powerful, but their power is limited in us
ing to our receptivity and faith.

- How have you experienced the healing power of the sacraments in your life?

- Do you remember a time when the "light switch" came on and you were able to believe and receive the graces in one or more of the sacraments?

- What impediments in your life currently keep you from opening your heart to the powerful healing graces inherent in the sacraments?

A few years after my CRHP experience, my brother Dave experienced his own personal healing and conversion, beginning on a CRHP weekend. While all the sacraments played a vital role in Dave's transformation, the two sacraments of healing—Penance and Anointing of the Sick—were particularly significant (CCC, 1421). Dave's initial restoration came through the Sacrament of Reconciliation on his CRHP weekend. His healing journey on earth culminated in the Sacrament of Anointing of the Sick, which he received two weeks before he died.

Like me, Dave began receiving the sacraments in infancy and received them with a modicum of faith until his teenage years. As altar boys, we often served Mass together, but after Dave started taking drugs in his teenage years, he went through a long period of being away from the Church. Like the prodigal son, Dave had almost completely squandered the inheritance he received in the Sacraments of Initiation (Baptism, Confirmation, and Eucharist). But as much as he ran away, the Father "had certainly not forgotten his son, indeed he had kept unchanged his affection and esteem for him."[6]

No matter how dark things became, Dave always had a sense of Jesus calling him back to the Father. I believe this was the hidden grace of the Holy Spirit working in his life, as a result of those sacraments he received early in life. For twenty long and troubled years, Dave ate out of the proverbial pigsty, before coming to his senses and heading back toward home (cf. Lk 15:17–20). At the age of thirty-five, Dave was released from jail and came to live with our family. Though our marriage was far from perfect, he could feel the love Margie and I had for each other, our daughters, and for him. Day after day he was being restored in very simple and ordinary ways, through conversations, meals, and simple acts of caring for him and each other. Looking back, I realize that Dave's healing process was aided by these graces flowing from our Sacrament of Matrimony. Almost imperceptibly, God was restoring Dave's security, which had been taken away in adolescence through our parents' divorce. Since adolescence, Dave had lived as a man without a home or family. For the first time in years, he could rest knowing he belonged and was being cared for in an intact family.

After six months of recuperation, Dave decided on his own that he wanted to attend a CRHP retreat weekend. By then, my brother Bart and our brother-in-law Nick had also participated in the process. Dave could see the fruit in each of our lives and was attracted to the peace we exuded. We were all amazed and excited when he expressed a desire to go himself, but we remained apprehensive, not knowing how he would respond. At the last minute, unworthiness and fear almost dissuaded him from going, but with a little encouragement, he ended up making it to church, where he was welcomed with open arms by our pastor and the other men on the team.

Strengthened by the graces of Holy Orders, Father Mike revealed the Father's love and acceptance in ways that Dave could tangibly see, hear, and feel. Because Father Mike's humble witness exalted Jesus and not himself, Dave immediately trusted him. As the weekend progressed and Dave heard Father Mike give personal witness to the power of the Sacrament of Reconciliation, Dave felt inspired to go to confession for the first time in twenty-five years. Father

Mike, representing the father in the parable of the prodigal son,[7] welcomed Dave with open arms and a compassionate heart, washing him clean through the sacrament. Incarnating the priesthood of Jesus Christ, Father Mike was able to offer Dave what no other human being could: the forgiveness of his sins through the precious blood of Jesus. In the celebration that followed in the Eucharist, Dave was clothed again in the finest robe of his sparkling baptismal garments in Christ. I am confident that all of heaven rejoiced in Dave's return (Lk 15:22–24), and Dave himself felt the joy and peace of a free heart, having been unburdened from the heavy weight of guilt he had been carrying. He felt loved and accepted for the first time in years, knowing that his worst sins were now confessed and out in the open.

When he finally got to bed, Dave was too excited to sleep. He stayed awake, reliving the incredible graces of the day. But his peaceful feeling soon turned to anguish and regret, as his thoughts took a turn for the worse. At this moment of great victory, the enemy of his soul came in like a thief, attempting to steal away the powerful graces of the day and accusing him of the very things he had just confessed. During the Sacrament of Reconciliation, the Holy Spirit assisted him in freely pouring out his sins, and Dave felt an exhilarating release. But now the reality of what he confessed came flooding back in, drowning him in a deluge of self-condemning thoughts and feelings, aided by an unholy spirit of self-hatred. He was bombarded by memory after memory of what he had done during those twenty years on the streets, including violent acts, robbery, and abandoning his daughter. All Dave could feel was an intense self-hatred. Doubting everything that had happened that evening, he was tempted to pack up and leave. These accusing and tempting thoughts continued incessantly: *None of this is real. I don't belong here. This isn't for me.*

Finally, not able to bear the tormenting thoughts any longer, he rolled off his cot and headed out of the sleeping area. Not sure where he was going, he found himself in the main sanctuary in front of the tabernacle. Kneeling before the altar and staring at the life-sized image of the Resurrected Jesus, he began to remonstrate with Jesus. *How can you forgive me after everything I have done? I don't deserve it. This may be for everyone else but not for me.* His diatribe continued until he exhausted himself. After spewing his self-hatred, Dave became quiet and his thoughts took a gentler turn. *Think about your family and how they have forgiven and accepted you. Where do you think that grace came from?* Dave was stopped in his tracks. Was this Jesus speaking to him? He began to feel a strange peace and calm invade his soul again.

Suddenly, Dave realized that everything he experienced that day came from Jesus, who is the only one fully capable of accepting and forgiving any of us. His death on the cross paid the price. It was finally all sinking in. For the first time in twenty-some years, Dave knew he was forgiven, loved, and accepted, in spite of everything he had done or failed to do. With these revelations, Dave's hardened heart was pierced and he began to sob, pouring out all the pain, guilt, and self-loathing that had accumulated through the years. It was like dirty water from a faucet, once clogged up, now suddenly released and becoming pure. The Father's mercy triumphed over all that had been so violently opposing it.

When we met Dave later that afternoon, he radiated the glory of God. Tears of joy sprang to my eyes as I saw his face, full of light and peace. I had my brother back. Even now, tears come to my eyes as I relive this memory. Later that evening when we had an opportunity to sit down together, he shared in more detail all that had happened during the retreat. I could not find words to adequately express my gratitude to the Father. I have learned since then that the Eucharist, which means "Great Thanksgiving," is the only adequate expression. "How can I repay the LORD for all the good done for me? I will raise the cup of salvation and call on the name of the LORD. . . . I will offer a sacrifice of thanksgiving. . . . Hallelujah!" (Ps 116:12–13, 17, 19).

As I recounted in the last chapter, Dave became a new man after his CRHP experience, but within a few years, he became progressively more infirm due to HIV. As we watched Dave declining both physically and mentally, our family earnestly prayed for his healing. But one night, I had a dream where I sensed the Holy Spirit saying: *You are praying for Dave's healing, but he is going to die with this illness. Through his dying process your entire family will receive much healing.*

Knowing that Dave was close to death, my sister Margaret and I traveled the three hours to visit him and my brother Wayne. When we arrived at Wayne's home, we were distraught to find Dave in a coma. Margaret and I had both hoped to have one last chance to say goodbye to Dave before he died. Disheartened and concerned that he might die any minute, we called a local priest (whom we didn't know) to give Dave the Sacrament of Anointing of the Sick. Dave remained unconscious as this priest prayed for him, and we all participated. After thanking the priest, Wayne, Margaret, and I decided to go for a run to plan Dave's funeral. The home health worker stayed behind in another room, leaving Dave alone in the bedroom.

After we finished our run and headed into the house, we were all startled by a magnificent sight: Dave was wide awake. He tried getting out of bed. We shouted for him to wait and ran into his bedroom. Overjoyed to see Dave awake again, we all gave him a big hug, all the while celebrating our own personal Lazarus experience (cf. John 11). Dave went on to tell us what happened. He said he felt himself slipping into death, but at the moment of the anointing he encountered Jesus in heaven. Jesus told him it was not yet time for him to come home and that there was something more for him to do.

Though Dave would live only another two weeks after receiving the sacrament, this resuscitation from death became a profound healing for many of us in the family and helped fulfill Dave's purpose of being someone with AIDS for Christ. That next afternoon, Dave's daughter, Sarah (then eight years old), and her mother came to say goodbye. We were all touched as we watched them interact with tender love and depart from one another while enveloped in super-natural peace.

After they left, Wayne, Margaret, and I gave Dave a bath. We laughed together and felt a bond of love as never before. It is a memory I will never forget, a moment of reliving the carefree baths of childhood. As we were leaving, we all expressed our deep love for Dave, not knowing whether we would see each other again on this side of heaven. When Dave hugged me, he held on for a long time, and said, "This is our best time together ever." I agreed. As a result of Dave's brief reprieve from the grips of death, several other family members had the opportunity to say goodbye to Dave. Over those final two weeks of Dave's life, my mom, her parents, her brother Sam, and my brother Bart all came to visit Dave. The crowning gift in the Father's providence came as Dad, Margie, and I were able to be with him in his final moments of life.

I will never again look at the Sacrament of Anointing of the Sick with indifference. I now see its two purposes clearly: (1) the restoration of health and (2) the preparation for passing over to eternal life (*CCC*, 1532).

Since these events, which occurred nearly twenty years ago, I have been growing progressively in my appreciation of the sacraments. I now realize that all of the sacraments are genuine encounters with the crucified and Risen Jesus. I love the way the current catechism defines these powerhouses of grace: "Sacraments are 'powers that come forth' from the Body of Christ which is ever-living and life-giving" (*CCC*, 1116).

I now realize that all of the sacraments are genuine encounters with the crucified and Risen Jesus.

The inspired writers of the catechism clearly had healing in mind when they wrote that definition, as the footnotes point to several of Jesus' healing encounters in the Gospel of Luke. Who is not captivated by the stories of Jesus healing the paralytic in body and soul, when his friends brought him down through the roof (Lk 5:17), or the woman who touched Jesus' garments and was healed of her longstanding infirmity (Lk 8:46)? How could I have ever believed the sacraments were boring? Nothing could be more exciting than these life-altering and healing encounters with Jesus, our Divine Physician (CCC, 1509).

But despite my new appreciation for what the sacraments are meant to be, my heart is still troubled by the ordinary experience of sacraments for many in the Church. How do I reconcile this beautiful understanding of the healing power of the sacraments with our typical celebrations of them in many churches? To be honest, my personal reception of the sacraments still looks a lot different than Jesus' healing miracles. When I read the scripture—"Power came forth from him and healed them all" (Lk 6:19b)—I have images of Jesus touching and healing many people, spiritually, physically, mentally, and in every possible way. But when I look at my own experiences with the sacraments, I am hard-pressed to find more than a few examples of this kind of miraculous healing. Why don't we see more evidence of this "power coming forth" in our communities and in each one of our personal lives? Is my faith still so impoverished? Has the entire body of Christ fallen asleep and become like the townspeople of Nazareth?

In his book *Evangelical Catholicism*, George Weigel attempts to awaken the sleeping giant. He fully appreciates the significance of sacraments being real encounters with the crucified and risen Jesus: "The seven sacraments . . . are seven privileged encounters with the Christ who is himself *the* sacramental expression of the living God in the world and in history. . . . The Word of God found in the Holy Scripture is encountered in the sacraments."[8]

If the sacraments really and truly are healing encounters with Jesus, we have to ask, where in our midst are the paralyzed getting up and walking? Where are the infirmed being cured? When I started asking these questions with a desire to find the answer, I found many remarkable testimonies of healing, which confirmed the Church's teaching. I discovered that Christ's life-giving and healing presence is particularly active in the Eucharist (CCC, 1509). Stories of Eucharistic miracles and healings abound throughout the history of the Church. Sister Briege McKenna recounts many stories of healing during the celebration of the Eucharist in her book *Miracles Do Happen*. One testimony that particularly touched me concerned a young boy with severe burns who was put under the altar at a Mass in Latin America and was completely and miraculously healed during the consecration.[9] More remarkable testimonies come from Father Robert DeGrandis and Linda Shubert, in their book *Healing through the Mass*, including this one from Ireland:

> A priest . . . explained in the gathering of 1,000 people that Jesus was wholly and completely present in the Eucharist and that in receiving His body and blood we should expect to be healed of our illnesses. The priest emphasized the need for Catholics to believe fully in his presence, his power and his desire to heal. During communion, sick and crippled people began jumping out of their chairs. I saw with my own eyes a mother crying as her baby's blindness was cured. The newspapers reported stories of old

women jumping out of wheelchairs and many varied illnesses healed.[10]

We see in these accounts the same kind of imagery that the catechism alludes to: power from Jesus, who is truly present in the sacraments, flowing out to heal many as people put their faith in him.

Christians throughout the world are testifying to healings they experience through the sacraments. Many of these are not Catholic but still have a deep respect for the graces inherent in the sacraments. One example comes from the ministry of Rolland and Heidi Baker. They testify to the amazing manifestations of Christ's healing power in their church in Mozambique, Africa, especially during Holy Communion and Baptism. What greater healing can there be than the one that occurs during every Baptism, when a new soul is born into eternal life? We only see the outward signs through the rituals of water, anointing, and exorcism. But occasionally, God gives evidence of the healing that is taking place. I personally know a woman who was healed of deafness when she was baptized.

In their book *There Is Always Enough*, the Bakers provide an amazing account of a young girl's healing through Baptism. I was moved to tears as I read of her trauma before she was adopted by the Bakers. Orphaned at the age of five after both her parents were brutally killed, she was so traumatized she did not speak. This is the Bakers' recounting of her Baptism: "When she came out of the water, she smiled for the first time among us. Her face radiated the glory of God. That day she suddenly began speaking again. . . . Later she told us that she had seen her parents shot and their heads cut off. . . . But Jesus came to her in the baptismal water and turned her mourning into joy."[11] These miraculous events are happening all over the world, confirming Jesus' real and life-giving presence in the sacraments, to his entire Church. Glory be to the Father, Son, and Holy Spirit! But despite all these miraculous events, you may still be wondering, as I have, How does this apply to our ordinary day-to-day lives? How can we appropriate the grace of the sacraments without needing to see miracles every time? Jesus told Thomas, "Blessed are those who have not seen and have believed" (Jn 20:29b).

TAKE A MOMENT

- What is your reaction when you read of these astounding healing experiences?

- Have you experienced healing in a specific area of your life through the sacraments?

Healing of Soul / mind / Body

Jesus' visible healings and miracles are awesome manifestations that build our faith in what we cannot see with our natural eyes. But more than anything, they serve as signs of a greater healing—our redemption from the effects of original sin. We have already noted that healing and redemption are synonymous. Our most desperate need for healing concerns our deepest wounds, those resulting from our separation from God. All that has been fractured by sin needs to be healed and restored. According to Pope Benedict XVI, this is the greatest healing that occurs through the sacraments: "The essence of original sin is the split into individuality. The essence of redemption is the mending of the shattered image of God, the union of the human race through the One [Jesus Christ] who stands in for all and in whom all are one. . . . Union is redemption."[12]

> *Jesus' visible healings and miracles are awesome manifestations that build our faith in what we cannot see with our natural eyes.*

Healing is communion. Sacramental grace is the power of Christ to bring us back into communion with the Father and with one another, through the Holy Spirit (CCC, 1153). In the Church's great wisdom, it realizes that all personal healing occurs in the context of a broader healing, the healing of relationships in family, church, and society. This broader relational healing occurs, in part, through what the Church calls "the Sacraments at the Service of Communion" (CCC, 1534): Holy Orders and Matrimony. The priesthood and marriage are two primary places where Jesus' image is to be revealed in the world (Eph 5:21–32).

These sacraments are such an ordinary part of our life that we often take them for granted. We don't pay much attention to them, until they are taken away. When my parents divorced and their marriage was later annulled, I realized the importance of good marriage preparation, so that married couples can establish a secure foundation for each other and their children.

I believe we take the Sacrament of Holy Orders for granted in similar ways, until we are without the daily sacrifice of our bishops, priests, and deacons. When we have a shortage of priests, our parishes close and sacraments are less available; only then do we begin to appreciate the gift we have been given by these men who have laid down their lives for us in the name of Christ.

Our public and personal outrage over dishonorable priests reveals even more how we value this sacrament without knowing it. The clergy sexual abuse scandals actually reveal the great dignity of the priesthood. Sexual abuse is a horrible betrayal of trust and innocence, which is going on in every segment of society, in school, in family life, and in our churches. We are rightly outraged at the damage that has been done. But notice when clergy are involved our outrage becomes magnified. The news becomes the featured headlines of our telecasts. Why? I believe it is because we consider betrayal by a priest to be the greatest betrayal in society. Whether conscious or not, everyone sees the priest as an image of Christ. They may not admit it, but their actions demonstrate it. Why else would they hold the priesthood to a higher standard and deserving greater scorn when violated?

Keeping all this in mind, let's revisit Pope Francis's remarks about the sacraments: "The grace contained in the Easter Sacraments is an enormous source of strength for renewal in personal and family life, as well as for social relations."[13] Do you see how critical the sacraments are to our overall healing? It is more than just seeing miracles of healing. It is the day-to-day strengthening of the social order that undergirds our lives. When these foundations of social life are diminished in value, social relations falter in direct proportion. As society continues to decline in morality, the brokenness and divisions in the Church keep it largely impotent. Christ's redeeming love, manifested through the sacraments, becomes weakened and ineffective.

This is why the movement of the Holy Spirit bringing unity and life back to the Church is so crucial in this hour. Only in unity and through the grace of the sacraments will the Church rise up and become the healing agent that Jesus commissioned her to be. And only through the restoration of the Church can our culture restore family life to the place God intends it, providing security, fostering maturity, and cultivating purity. All of this is so much bigger than our individual healing. The sacraments are Christ's healing offered to the whole person, the whole family, the whole Church, and the whole world.

How could I have ever believed the sacraments are mundane? There is nothing boring about the sacraments. They are truly "powers coming forth from the body of Christ," not just for our individual healing, but also for the healing of all of our relationships and society at large. They are not magic rites but are nevertheless powerful healing encounters with Jesus. These powerful graces are available to us at all times.

Pause and try to envision your life without the sacraments.

- How would your life be different without the sacraments? How would that affect your eternal life?

- Do you encounter Jesus in the sacraments? Explain why or why not.

- Create a list of things that would help you to become more open to receiving these healing graces in your life?

Persistent prayer, fortified by an intimate relationship with Jesus, is the key to opening our hearts to receive the abundant graces inherent in the sacraments. This will be our emphasis in the next chapter, "Healing Prayer."

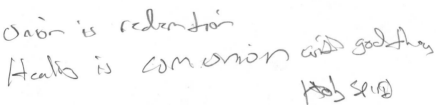

All Sacraments are encounters
with Jesus) Heals

Order   Communion
Matrimony   Penance
Ointing of Sick   Baptism
                               Confirmation

Union is redemption
Heals is comunion and godthy
                          Holy Spirit

CHAPTER TEN

HEALING PRAYER

*Jesus has awakened great hopes. . . . He has shown the face
of God's mercy, he has bent down to heal body and soul.*

Pope Francis,
Palm Sunday, 2013

The Acts of the Apostles begins with the disciples hidden away in
the Upper Room, in prayer. After nine days of concerted interces-
sion, the Holy Spirit descends upon them, manifesting his powerful
presence in and through them. In one startling morning, the world
is changed forever, as the Gospel is proclaimed to representatives of
all the nations. Our own faith is the result of the great harvest that
began that day.

As a result of this encounter with the Holy Spirit the disciples'
lives were radically transformed. As chronicled by Pope John Paul
II in the *Splendor of Truth*, the Holy Spirit empowered and embold-
ened them for all that would be required of them. "Strengthened
by his gift, they did not fear prisons or chains for the name of the
Lord; indeed they even trampled upon the powers and torments of
the world, armed and strengthened by him, having in themselves
the gifts which the same Spirit bestows and directs like jewels to the
Church, the Bride of Christ."[1]

The jewels that Pope John Paul II refers to are the gifts of the Spirit, which are given not only to the disciples but to each of us as well. The Church was built and continues to be built through these gifts of supernatural empowerment. Among these spiritual gifts are multiform gifts of healing and miracles (1 Cor 12:9). When the disciples prayed for the sick, they were healed. They even called the dead back to life just as they saw their teacher do. They knew it was not in their power to do any of these things, but they trusted in the name of Jesus and in the power of the Holy Spirit working through them (Acts 3:6).

Come Holy
Spirit give me
the Strength ——>

At Pentecost the Holy Spirit rushed upon the disciples in tongues of fire. This fire is God's blazing love and life-altering power that continues burning in the Church today.[2] Whether we realize it or not, this fire is the longing of every human being. In the words of Pope Benedict XVI, "The ultimate thirst of men cries out for the Holy Spirit."[3]

Don't you long to live with the same kind of vitality and boldness as the apostles did after Pentecost? This fire of God's love and power is already deposited within us, by virtue of our Baptism and Confirmation. In fact, the catechism calls the Sacrament of Confirmation "a full outpouring of the Holy Spirit as once granted to the apostles on the day of Pentecost" (*CCC*, 1302). And Father Raniero Cantalamessa adds, "The power which is the Holy Spirit, still *now* comes out of Jesus. . . . This power heals *everybody*."[4]

Let those words inspire and challenge you. We have the same gifts as the apostles after Pentecost. Everywhere the Holy Spirit is given permission in our hearts, the love of God heals us and brings us and others into greater freedom (2 Cor 3:17). Like the early disciples, we too are called to go near and far as his representatives, enflamed by his fire burning within us. We are called to set the nations ablaze with God's love and to allow that purifying fire to burn out all our infirmities, bringing God's light into the deepest darkness that inhabits men's souls (Mk 16:17–18; Is 61:1–4).

We have the same gifts as the apostles after Pentecost.

Though full of fire and passion, the Holy Spirit is also a gentle power. He will not force himself; he must be welcomed and received. Notice that before the gift was given at Pentecost, Jesus told the disciples to prepare their hearts. They waited on the Holy Spirit in prayer. They could neither earn nor manipulate this gift, but their participation was vital. As I study this account, three elements of their cooperation stand out to me, because these are also present in all prayers for healing:

1. The disciples *trusted* Jesus and followed his direction.
2. They *prayed* from the depths of their *hearts* (see CCC, 2562–63).
3. They were *united* in mind and heart (Phil 2:1–2).

The disciples did not sit back and wait passively but actively entreated the heavens for the promised Holy Spirit, engaging their wills in expectant faith and trusting fully in Jesus' promise. Isn't this what the Church is all about? And yet, what is our standard fare? We often resemble Jesus' disciples *before* Pentecost, who had a hard time believing Jesus really meant what he said. Do we really trust his words when he says, "If you ask anything of me in my name, I will do it" (Jn 14:14)? As a direct consequence of denying the power of God available to us in Christ, we lack faith and thereby fail to pray. When we do pray, it is often halfhearted.

I believe one of the reasons for this halfheartedness is our lack of hope and trust that God will hear us, that he will answer us when we call out to him. We sometimes fear that the Father will not give us what we have requested. After all, not everyone is healed when and how we expect.

Yielding to the Spirit in prayer is always a vulnerable experience. It is somewhat like the man who is hanging over a cliff, holding onto a branch. Realizing he has no other choice, he cries out to God to save him. When he hears a voice from the ground say, "Let go," he asks, "Is there anyone else down there?" We may laugh, but we are often like that man. We ask for God's help but sometimes find it terrifying to let go of our agendas and control. As I shared in chapter 3, praying for healing can challenge us to the core. We must continually "let go and let God" without any guarantee that the people to whom we are ministering will receive the healing they so desperately need and desire.

When Prayers for Healing Appear Unanswered

Even those most anointed with gifts of healing know the pain of praying for someone who is not healed. In his book *The Power to Heal*, Francis MacNutt estimates that about 25 percent of the people he prays with experience radical and nearly instantaneous healings, while another 50 percent report that they experience partial healing. Isn't it amazing that 75 percent receive some healing?[5] But what about the other 25 percent who go away with their hopes dashed? I know from experience how difficult this can be for all involved.

This past year, I was invited to pray for two people with terminal cancer: one was a six-year-old girl with a brain tumor; the other, a wife and mother of a large family, who homeschooled young children. They were both too young to die, and both had family that desperately wanted and needed them to live. But despite all of our hopes and many prayers, both prayer recipients died. Their families, still grieving the loss of their loved ones, are left wondering why Jesus did not heal them. After experiences such as these, it is tempting for everyone to quit praying, thinking it is either too risky or a waste of time. But I have learned to trust that where God's love is present, healing is always taking place.

In both of these situations, we may have lost the battle against the evil of cancer, but Jesus still ultimately came out victorious. The parents of the dying young girl both received deep inner healing and experienced an outpouring of the Holy Spirit in our time of prayer together. Before the woman died, she and her husband experienced a beautiful healing in their marital relationship during our prayer time. The greatest healing of all came in a way none of us could see with our human eyes: the two prayer recipients ended up meeting Jesus face to face in heaven. This is the ultimate healing. The enemy won two battles, but in the bigger picture Jesus conquered overwhelmingly.

What I have learned in situations like these is to keep my focus on Jesus. If we are listening to the voice of our Good Shepherd, he will guide us how to pray for others. Even when we do not see the immediate effects of our prayers, we need to keep praying, unless Jesus tells us to stop (assuming he led us to begin praying in the first place). Many of those 75 percent mentioned by Francis MacNutt who do not receive immediate healing may still be healed as we persevere in prayer.

Persistence in Prayer

Jesus emphasized the need for us to persist in prayer until we receive our answer (Lk 18:1–8), exhorting us to ask and keep on asking, seek and keep on seeking, and knock and keep on knocking (Lk 11:9). Jesus himself had to pray with a particular blind man more than once (Mk 8:22–26), and many of us in the healing ministry are realizing that repeated prayer, far from reflecting a lack of faith, produces amazing results.

Remember Daniel in the Old Testament, who prayed for twenty-one days before he got his answer from the Lord's messenger: "Fear not, Daniel . . . from the first day . . . your prayer was heard. Because of it, I started out, but the prince of the kingdom of Persia stood in my way for twenty-one days, until finally Michael, one of the chief princes, came to help me" (Dn 10:12–13).

Daniel's prayer was heard by God immediately, but he didn't receive his answer for twenty-one days, after a considerable spiritual battle. Like Daniel, when we enter into prayer, we too are engaged in spiritual warfare (Eph 6:12; *CCC*, 2725). God responds to our prayer for healing quickly, but his answer is often opposed by the enemy who tries to keep us in bondage under his control and to lead us to give up hope. After being with Jesus, the disciples learned this lesson well. They understood that healing involved freeing those oppressed by the devil (Acts 10:38). Remember, behind all our scientific explanations, evil is at the root of everything that afflicts us. Francis MacNutt adds to this understanding of why we need to persevere in prayer: "This much has become abundantly clear: prayer for healing is often a process. It requires time."[6]

> In all of us there are areas where sickness, sluggishness, and death are at work spiritually, emotionally, and physically. But when another Christian or a community gathers around to pray, the life, the love, and the healing power of Jesus can be transmitted to the sick person. If there is a great deal of sickness . . . it may take *time* for the radiating power of Jesus to begin to dissolve [the ailment]. It is like God's radiation treatment.[7]

As we step out in faith to pray, we can be assured that our Father will give good gifts to his children. When we ask for a fish, he will not give us a snake (Lk 11:11–13). With this confidence we are able to persist in prayer, believing that healing will come, whether quickly or more gradually.

I saw the amazing results of persistent prayer a few months before going to Brazil. Sitting with a small group of Christians in our monthly Christ-centered Family Reconstruction community, I discovered that two of the women present had been on a prayer team in Londrina, Brazil, the very city of my upcoming mission trip. One woman, Sally, who had recently returned from the mission trip, passed around a picture of a young girl who had been healed of spina bifida. She then relayed how she felt led to consistently and persistently pray for this little girl for two days, ten hours each day.

I don't know if I would have had the faith or persistence to pray that long, but somehow by the grace of God, she did. And an amazing miracle of healing resulted. After twenty hours, the young girl was completely healed and her spinal column was restored to wholeness. When Sally passed around the picture and shared her story with our community, each person in the room

"A prayer that calls for an extraordinary action must be a prayer that involves all of us, as though our very life depends on it. In prayer, you have to put yourself to the test."

delighted in seeing the little girl's exuberant smile. But I noticed that when I looked around the room, one woman was crying, not out of sadness, but in amazement and gratitude to Jesus. She couldn't believe what she was seeing and hearing. This woman, Brenda, went on to tell all of us that a year earlier, when she was in Brazil, she had also prayed for hours for this same little girl. She was so moved with hope and faith for this precious child that she brought her picture home and put it on her refrigerator, praying for her every day for a year and believing she would be healed.

These women had the same fighting spirit as Pope Francis seems to have, as he exhorted all of us in a homily at a daily mass to develop this kind of perseverance in prayer: "A prayer that calls for an extraordinary action must be a prayer that involves all of us, as though our very life depends on it. In prayer, you have to put yourself to the test."[8] This kind of perseverance is an amazing gift of grace. It does not come naturally or easily. In my years of praying with people and in my own personal healing journey, I have discovered that many of us give up way too easily. Part of the reason for our resignation is that we end up running into impediments that block the grace invoked by our prayers.

Barriers to Healing

Do you remember how many of the stories of healing throughout this book involved barriers that had to be overcome? For example, when my team and I prayed for the two women in Brazil who had been sexually abused, we discovered many invisible strongholds that these women had unwittingly constructed to protect their broken hearts. These impediments to their healing were formed, often unconsciously, through inner vows, judgments, and identity lies, covering their wounds of shame, hopelessness, and abandonment. Similarly, the young girl whose leg was damaged in the accident had barriers of fear and un-forgiveness that had to be addressed before she could receive the graces from our prayers. In John's situation, the barriers to his healing involved his inability and unwillingness to face the deep pain of abandonment, as well as judgments, vows, and identity lies. Each of those situations required perseverance in prayer and docility to the Holy Spirit, who showed us how to overcome these obstacles in prayer.

Overcoming Obstacles in Prayer

In the process of praying for ourselves and others, we must regularly contend with the "thief and robber" who comes after Jesus' flock, to rob, kill, and destroy (Jn 10:1–4). Our minds and hearts are often the primary battlefield.[9] The most difficult battle in prayer comes in relation to the strongholds that have already taken root inside us, in our own minds and hearts. Both the seven deadly sins and the seven deadly wounds give the enemy authority in specific areas of our lives. These fortresses of self-will and self-protection, undergirded by our beliefs and vows, eventually become expressed in maladaptive behaviors and poor health.

To be effective, healing prayer must uproot the specific identity lies and other barriers that hold these strongholds in place.[10] This is why we spent so much time going through the detailed description of strongholds in part two.

TAKE A MOMENT

Think back for a moment and reflect on the anatomy of a wound in chapter 7. Do you remember the three concentric circles from figure 7.1 (p. 113)?

- What were your core wounds? Can you write out the identity beliefs associated with them?

- What judgments toward yourself, others, and God did you discover?

- Were you able to see where you made inner vows to protect yourself?

Each of these barriers can interfere with us receiving the healing we desire and God desires for us. The following example illustrates:

- If you have a wound of *abandonment*, it is very likely that you have a deeply held belief that no one hears or understands you. My experience suggests that deep down you may also believe that God has abandoned you and does not hear your prayers. If that is the case, you may pray halfheartedly or give up when you meet the first sign of resistance or delay. All the while you may rationalize this to yourself with thoughts such as, *Maybe Jesus doesn't want to heal this*. But if you listen carefully to the Holy Spirit, you will find that these are deceptions lurking in the darkness, discouraging you from praying.
- Suppose in your experience of abandonment you made an inner vow: *I will not look to anyone else for help. I will take care of myself*. With this silent resolution, perhaps formed in your heart at a young age, you may not even think about praying.

Instead, you may just try to solve things on your own, trying to cope with whatever ails you.

I regularly encounter these barriers in prayer, in myself and when praying for others. A typical example of this occurred several years ago when I was praying with a woman who had been conceived out of wedlock. She did not know her father and later found out her mother had been raped. The daughter, married with children of her own, harbored major wounds of rejection and abandonment her entire life. She believed she was "a mistake" and "dirty" because of how she was conceived. She never felt loved or wanted but always felt as if she had ruined her mother's life and thus everyone else's. These identity lies kept her bound in shame.

When we asked the Holy Spirit to show us the roots underlying her wounds, she was shown a vision (in her imagination) of her mother being raped. As she looked on as an objective observer, her attention was drawn up to heaven where she saw a dove (representing the Holy Spirit) come down from heaven and bring life to her mother's womb. Instantly, she realized that even though she was unplanned by her mother and conceived by her father's sin, she was ultimately alive because of God's choice and power. For the first time in her life, she believed in her heart that she was a gift from the Lord and Giver of Life. The Holy Spirit then showed her many things about her purpose, destiny, and the future of her family in heaven.

At the end of the prayer experience, we went back and tested whether she still believed the identity lies that had plagued her throughout her life. In examining, we discovered that these lies around her conception were completely gone. The seven signs of healing shown in table 10.1, which can be used as a way of testing the validity of inner healing prayer, were evident in her life, replacing the identity lies and wounds.

Table 10.1. Seven signs of healing

7 DEADLY WOUNDS	7 SIGNS OF HEALING
Abandonment	Connected and understood
Rejection	Accepted and valued
Fear	Safe and secure
Shame	Pure and worthy
Powerlessness	Empowered and liberated
Hopelessness	Hopeful and encouraged
Confusion	Clarity and enlightenment

This woman knew in her heart without a shadow of a doubt that God wanted her alive and that she was not a mistake; she felt *connected* and *safe*, with a new sense of her own *purity* and *freedom*. She left our prayer time with renewed *hope* and *clarity*. After receiving her healing, she knew that her life was willed by God. She saw clearly how the Holy Spirit had worked even in the midst of her father's violent sin to bring her into the world. She also knew that she was wanted and loved by her heavenly Father, by her husband and children, and by many others. For the first time, her life had purpose and meaning. Even though this woman still struggled in other areas of her life after this prayer, this particular stronghold was broken, and she was free to give and receive love in a new way, with renewed joy and hope. With increased freedom and confidence, she could now pray to the Father and believe that he heard and answered her prayers.

We all desire this kind of fruit in our lives, don't we? We want to know that we are loved and accepted, understood and connected to the people we love. We want to live with greater hope and freedom and have vision and clarity in our lives. We yearn to be freed from the strongholds in our lives resulting from our wounds and deadly sins. In short, we all want to come to a deeper knowledge of our identity as the Father's beloved and to give and receive love with greater abandon.

The Father has not left us as orphans, living in servile fear and self-reliance. He has given us the priceless gift of prayer, access to his heart at any time of day or night. I want to invite you now to consider a time when you received healing of your identity from an encounter with Jesus in prayer.

TAKE A MOMENT

Reflect on an area of your life where you experienced healing.

- Describe the identity lie that you believed before the healing experience.

- How did Jesus answer you?

- Were there any barriers that had to be overcome? What were they?

- After the healing experience, how were the seven signs of healing manifested in your life?

The Many Forms of Prayer

Healing does not depend on any particular method or form of prayer. The only requirements are an open heart and our willingness to be docile to the Holy Spirit. "According to Scripture it is the *heart* that prays. . . . only the Spirit of God can fathom the human heart and know it fully. . . . The heart is . . . the place of encounter" (*CCC*, 2562–2563).

A healing encounter with Jesus, in the power of the Holy Spirit, can take place through any number of prayer methods. In his book

New Outpourings of the Spirit, Cardinal Ratzinger (Pope Benedict XVI) showed how the various renewal movements in the history of the Church have encouraged the faithful to remain continually open to the multifold manifestations of the Holy Spirit. As a result, these movements revitalize our prayers. Each of these movements have added different insights and methods of prayer, building on the basic foundations of intercessory prayer, meditative prayer, and contemplative prayer that have been practiced in the Church throughout her history (see *CCC*, 559; *CCC*, 2721).

For example, the Jesuits have their own unique way of teaching us how to pray that is different from the Carmelites, and the Carmelites' method of praying is in turn distinct from the Dominicans, the Salesians method, and so on. In recent years, the charismatic and liturgical movements have also offered the Church many new forms and methods of prayer, while preserving the traditional ones. Together these movements make up the rich tradition of the Church, all the while keeping it ever docile to the Holy Spirit. I find it helpful to borrow from all of these prayer movements, making sure to allow the Holy Spirit to lead, without becoming too wedded to any one method.

A personal prayer experience of mine many years ago illustrates how these various methods of prayer can be employed together, with the guidance of the Holy Spirit. In this specific instance, the Lord was showing me some of the roots underlying my pride but in such a gentle way that I didn't even realize he was performing this delicate surgery in my soul. I began by being drawn into a time of *listening prayer*, where I encountered Jesus through the scriptures. I reflected on the insights I received from the Holy Spirit by writing them in a journal. As I attended to the various passages, one in particular jumped out at me, from the epistle of James: "God resists the proud, but gives grace to the humble" (Jas 4:6b). From there, the Spirit led me to many other passages about pride and humility; many I had read before, but this time they spoke to me in a new way, as I began reflecting on them in meditative prayer.

In the middle of my journaling, I was "interrupted" by a phone call from my friend Wyatt, who was away on a business trip. He told me he had been praying for me (intercessory prayer) and shared several of the scripture passages that he was receiving. You may have guessed: The Holy Spirit led him to some of the same scripture passages I had been receiving in my prayer time. When I got off the phone, I went back to prayer, thanking the Father for my good friend and confirming what I had been receiving in journaling with such clarity. In the midst of my prayer (of thanksgiving), I was "interrupted" again but this time by an image that came into my mind unexpectedly (contemplative prayer).

This image I received from the Holy Spirit portrayed me running around a track with a crowd of people cheering me on. I was surprised by this image and thought the Lord was using it to reveal specific roots of my pride, since sports had been one of the areas of my self-idolatry. But as I continued to look and listen, I realized that was not his message at all; track was my least favorite sport, and few people ever showed up to watch our track meets.

As I continued searching for the meaning of this image, I sensed the Holy Spirit asking me to look up into the crowd. When I did, I saw (in my inspired imagination) the "great cloud of witnesses" (Heb 12:1). I quickly discovered that the track represented my life journey; I was running the race of faith and being freed from the "burden and sin that clings to us" (Heb 12:1). I had an inward knowing that among the "cloud of witnesses" the Trinity, angels and saints, and my relatives in heaven were all present, cheering me on and praying for me (intercessory prayer).

Now basking in the presence of God's glory, I felt completely loved and accepted for the first time in my life. For that brief moment, I sensed the complete absence of pride. All the seven signs of healing were present. I felt *empowered* and *pure*, full of *hope* and *understanding*. In the presence of this "great cloud of witnesses" I felt *understood* and *deeply connected* as never before in my life. It was a real taste of heaven. I had no need to impress anyone or get anyone's approval, as I felt totally *accepted* and *valued* in their presence. This unconditional love, given to me as a pure gift, couldn't be earned by any of my performances, gifts, or talents.

In light of this encounter, I became aware of some of the deeper underlying wounds beneath my sins of pride and vainglory. These wounds of rejection, shame, and abandonment had followed me most of my life. In believing I was unloved, unlovable, and alone, I unconsciously chose pride as a vain attempt to make myself lovable. I hid my fears and inadequacy behind my abilities. In this moment I realized it was all vainglory.

This experience in prayer proved to be a real eye-opener. It was my first conscious experience with contemplative prayer, and it came as a complete grace. Experiencing freedom from all these strongholds gave me a greater hunger and thirst for heaven, where we are all loved fully and never alone. I realized at that moment that I will have no pride in heaven. It all started when I followed the Holy Spirit's lead in prayer, drawing on scripture and journaling what he was showing me. Would you like to try it yourself?

TAKE A MOMENT

I invite you now to spend some time in prayer. Let the Holy Spirit lead you into an encounter with Jesus and the Father. If you don't know where to begin, start with scripture, perhaps with some of the scriptures we have been drawing from in this book. Open your heart and let yourself be drawn into the passages as though you were one of the people in the scene. Do you feel called to be the woman at the well (Jn 4), the lame man beside the pool of Bethesda (Jn 5), the woman caught in adultery (Jn 8), or the blind Bartimaeus (Mk 10:46–52)? Perhaps it is a different image; let the Spirit lead you by your desires and be open to whatever he shows you. Then record all that is spoken in a notebook or journal.

As you complete the time of prayer, try to write out the following:

- What did you experience in your prayer time?
- What did you believe about yourself?
- Did you encounter Jesus? What happened?
- Did you face any barriers? How did Jesus address these?
- Did you experience healing in the process?
- Which of the seven signs of healing were present when you finished?
- After prayer, do you experience a greater freedom? Describe it.
- Write out a prayer thanking Jesus for what he showed you.

One of the most telling indicators that we have received healing in our body, soul, and spirit is an increased awareness of a new interior freedom. This will be our focus in our concluding chapter, "Living in Freedom."

CONCLUSION: LIVING IN FREEDOM

In reality, freedom is a great gift only when we know how to use it consciously for everything that is our true good.

Pope John Paul II,
The Redeemer of Man

Freedom is a great gift. The desire for it is written deeply within each of our hearts. And yet, we often exercise our liberty in ways that do not bring about our true and lasting good. As a result we are left imprisoned, bound up in shame and hiding behind walls of fear and self-protection. We remain driven by our wounds and compulsions and become slaves of sin.

This universal story has been reflected in the individual stories of the people you have met in the previous chapters. This is our common broken human condition—we are all fallen and desperately in need of Christ's redemption. We need his healing to release us "from slavery to corruption" so that we can share in "the glorious freedom of the children of God" (Rom 8:21).

Freedom for its own sake is wonderful but not enough. We must learn how "to use it consciously for everything that is our true good."[1] Being set free from strongholds (the seven deadly sins and seven deadly wounds) is a great freedom, but it cannot be our ultimate goal. We must exercise our newfound freedom for the good of everyone around us and ultimately for the glory of God.

As we have said in many ways throughout this book, our wounds come from ruptured relationships with God, ourselves, and others. When these ruptures are healed, we can live in the freedom of the Holy Spirit as the Father's beloved sons and daughters. Healing is communion. This is the only true and lasting freedom, the kind that blesses others and never considers using them.

This glorious liberty allows us to see others and know who they are and what they need. We become capable of pursuing the good of those around us and in the process discover the greatest possible good for ourselves: our dignity and our purpose. Pope John Paul II was fond of quoting the Second Vatican Council in this regard: "Man

Healing is communion.

. . . cannot fully find himself without making a sincere gift of himself."[2] Our true freedom comes as we learn how to receive God's love and then give it away. This is the glorious liberty that the young man John eventually experienced after a long and difficult struggle with his sexual compulsions.

Do you remember John's story from chapter seven? I promised I would tell you the rest of his story before we finished, as it beautifully illustrates our common spiritual journey from slaves (of sin, wounds, and compulsions) into "the glorious freedom of the children of God" (Rom 8:21).

If you recall, when I first met John he had recently experienced a powerful healing encounter with Jesus during a college retreat. He found substantial freedom from his addiction to alcohol and drugs, and dedicated himself to serving God with much enthusiasm. But even after his life-changing encounter, John remained enslaved by a compulsive sexual addiction that had plagued him for many years. Though he continued to draw much strength from the sacraments, there was still something holding him back. Even after his pastor encouraged him to see me for therapy, John made little progress. Finally, we fasted and prayed together, and the Holy Spirit directed us to explore John's sexual fantasies as a way to discover the root issues underlying his compulsion.

When we prayed, the Holy Spirit uncovered a memory of John, as a two-year-old, watching his mother breastfeed his sister. We both saw how John had closed his heart to his mother at that tender age and vowed never to need anything from her again. In that same imaginative prayer experience, Jesus came to John and carried him to Mary (Jesus' mother), who nurtured the little boy John. The experience for John seemed very real, manifesting in a release of deeply held pain and shame he had been carrying most of his life.

Following our time of prayer, John and I both believed that he had been completely set free from his sexual compulsion. As we tested it over the next several months. As a result, we both felt at peace about John terminating therapy. This coincided with his graduation and decision to move to another city. We both wrongly assumed that John had been set free for good. But if you recall, there was a missing piece of the puzzle that didn't make sense at the time. It all became a lot clearer when John called me ten years later.

I had been wondering how John was doing and also wanted to get his permission to share his story with others. But I didn't have any way of contacting him. I knew he lived out of town but had no idea where. Providentially, I received a phone call from John. He told me he had been thinking about me and wanted to tell me the rest of the story of what had happened to him since we met.

After some general catching up, John filled in the missing details. He revealed that after our last meeting, he experienced freedom from his sexual compulsions for over a year. He talked about how good it felt to be free and how much he had grown during that time. But he admitted that his relationship with his mother did not improve and something inside kept telling him he wasn't fully free and would fall again. And sure enough he did fall—in a big way.

This time, the compulsion came roaring back worse than ever, along with his old addictions to alcohol and drugs. My heart sank when John recounted his living hell. I thought about the passage where Jesus warned that the demons would come back seven times worse if the space is left vacant (Mt 12:43–45). I felt devastated for him and wondered how this could have happened when we both believed he had been set free. John continued,

> I knew that day in your office there was another piece of memory that needed healing, but I wasn't ready to deal with it. That is why I was crying so hard in our prayer time. The memory I couldn't face involved the day my mother left when I was one and a half years old. Her mother was dying in another country, and she left for six weeks. I cried and didn't understand why she was leaving me. By the time she returned, my heart had completely closed to her. It hurt too much to need anything from her. That is when I made my vow to "never want anything from her again." From that point on, until about six years ago, I hated my mother.

John's turning point came when he got fed up with being miserable and begged Jesus to deliver him. Soon after his prayer of desperation, the Father placed someone in his life who could pray with him, in a similar way that we prayed together in my office. Realizing that he could not overcome his compulsions and addictions without facing his deeper wounds and pain, he was willing to address the haunting memory from which he had been running. The following is a paraphrase of what John told me about his second prayer experience:

> In my prayer time, I saw it all clearly in my memory. My mom was walking out the door, my dad was saying good-bye, and I was lying on the ground by myself feeling totally alone. This time Jesus didn't come to me but went to my mother instead. I couldn't believe it; I was furious and started throwing a temper tantrum. But Jesus, seeing my mother's pain, went over to her and put his hand on her shoulder. As soon as Jesus touched my mom, I could see this amazing look of compassion on his face. His love for my mother was incredible. At that moment, all my hatred for my mother dissolved. I could finally forgive her, realizing this was not something she wanted but had to do. I saw how much it hurt her to leave me. Since that moment all my anger and bitterness vanished. Now I love my mom. We have a great relationship, and I have a great relationship with my sister too.

The shift in John's heart toward his mother and sister allowed him to receive many more graces. As he was freed from his deep wounds, his compulsions lost their force. Since that day, he said he no longer feels the need to medicate his pain or fantasize about the love he could never get. He opened his heart to love his mother and sister, and soon after this event, he met a woman who would eventually become his wife. They are now happily married, enjoying their children and extended family and sharing a mutual love for Jesus. Facing his pain and forgiving his mother from his heart were the keys to John's healing, as they are to all of ours.

John's story reminded me once again that true forgiveness is the key to so much of our healing (see Mt 18:35). Betty Tapscott and Father Robert DeGrandis in their book *Forgiveness and Inner Healing* express it well:

> God wants you to be free. He wants to heal you—spirit, soul, and body. However, we can never be completely free and healed until we forgive. Forgiveness is the foundation for all healing. . . . Many times un-forgiveness is also accompanied by hate, resentment, revenge, anger, and bitterness. If we allow these negative emotions to remain in our spirits, we perhaps will end up with a physical problem, such as arthritis, high blood pressure, stomach problems, colitis, or heart problems.[3]

Forgiving from the heart is good for our health. It is also the key to healing sexual compulsions, addictions to alcohol and drugs, broken relationships, anxiety, depression, and so on, as we have witnessed through the stories in this book. Behind most of our physical and psychological ailments are these spiritual root issues, which must be addressed for full healing to take place. Even when we, like John, believe we are healed, these bitter roots can still defile us and bring us back into spiritual and emotional bondage (Heb 12:15). We cannot shortcut the road to healing. Jesus made this very clear when he said, "If you remain in my word, you will truly be my disciples, and you will know the truth, and the truth will set you free" (Jn 8:31–32). Pope John Paul II explains,

> The man is certainly free inasmuch as he can understand and accept God's commands. And he possesses an extremely far-reaching freedom, since he can eat of "every tree of the garden." But his freedom is not unlimited; it must halt before the "tree of knowledge of good and evil," for it is called to accept the moral law given by God. . . . God, who alone is good, knows perfectly what is good for man.[4]

This wisdom from the scriptures and Church teaching now means something to John. He no longer desires the false freedom that says: I can do anything I want, as long as I don't get caught. He has experienced his fill of the fruit from the tree of knowledge of good and evil, and it has made him sick. Though this fruit is still sometimes "pleasing to the eyes" (Gn 3:6), he remembers the bitter taste, and it repulses him.

Gaining a greater understanding of his own personal "tree of knowledge," John is much more aware of how his personal sins and wounds fueled his compulsions and how these have played out in his life. All of the *seven deadly sins* (pride, anger, envy, greed, sloth, gluttony, and lust) fed his compulsions and addictions. The bad fruit from each of these deadly sins poisoned his mind and heart and nearly destroyed his life.

Underlying these symptoms were the *seven deadly wounds* (abandonment, rejection, shame, fear, powerlessness, hopelessness, and confusion). These wounds emerged in part from his experience of abandonment from his mother. He also felt abandoned by his father, who didn't see and understand his hurt. Unaddressed, these wounds became the hard soil for roots of bitterness to spring up in his heart, culminating in judgments toward his mother, father, and sister. To cope with all this, John vowed at a young age that he would take care of himself and comfort himself. Alcohol and sex were two of the means he used to soothe his pain and anxiety. By the time he was twelve, these were habitual vices in his life.

In John's healing process, he needed to face the pain of these wounds so that he could overcome the bitter roots and forgive his parents and sister from the depths of his heart. He had tried forgiving them before, but the healing never reached the depths of his hurt. Facing the pain of abandonment is probably the most difficult thing John has ever done. But he now realizes how necessary it was for him to walk through it with Jesus as a means of redemptive suffering in order to experience the freedom of resurrection life.

Can you imagine how much pain he would have caused his wife and children without allowing these deadly sins to be crucified with Christ? His willingness to face his suffering before marriage continues to be a great gift to his family. He now understands the necessity in marriage of laying his life down for his wife and children as a sacrificial offering in communion with Jesus (Eph 5:25).

Having experienced the degradation of sex, John now places a high value on the Sacrament of Matrimony and fidelity with his spouse. In fact, he is deeply grateful for all the ways he has encountered Jesus through the sacraments. They have played a major role in his healing process. John's healing journey began by encountering Jesus in the Sacraments of Reconciliation and Eucharist, and since that beginning, he continues to be strengthened through them.

John has a great appreciation for the gift of Holy Orders, which makes the other sacraments available. He is especially grateful to the priest who walked with him through his worst times, laying down his life for John in very practical ways. By offering John spiritual direction and the Sacrament of Reconciliation, he incarnated Jesus' merciful love and showed John the compassionate face of the Father. Through this priest's spiritual fathering, John found a safe environment in which he could face his sin without fearing further condemnation.

John also appreciates the many people who, empowered by the Holy Spirit through the Sacrament of Confirmation, relied on the gifts of the Spirit to bring him into deeper freedom and healing. Healing prayer is obviously something very dear to John's heart, as his powerful encounters with Jesus in imaginative prayer have brought about a liberation that he could never fathom on his own. He experienced significant breakthroughs as he saw "Jesus walk hand in hand with him . . . during unpleasant situations and times of trauma."[5] He found peace and communion in the depths of his heart, through the Holy Spirit (see CCC, 2714).

John still practices this way of praying with scripture and in his personal prayer time. In addition, he and his wife pray the Rosary together, entering into the mysteries of Christ's life and applying it to their life circumstances together. This prayer keeps them grounded in truth and strengthened with the conviction that they can endure whatever they need to face.

Drawing on all these means of healing—prayer, sacraments, and redemptive suffering—John is growing in confidence that he is a beloved son of the Father. He is finding his identity in the Father who sees everything and everyone with eyes of mercy. As a result, John is learning to abide in the tree of life, enjoying its many and abundant fruits. Figure 11.1 on the *Healing Tree of Life* summarizes John's healing process and provides a blueprint for each of ours.

Starting at the bottom of the tree, notice the seven signs of healing, next to the word *security*. By overcoming the deep pain and burdensome shame he carried for much of his life, John now enjoys a freedom that he never believed possible. Since Jesus uprooted rejection from his heart, he now believes that he is loved and accepted. Whereas isolation and abandonment once dominated his life and fueled his addictions, he now largely feels connected and understood. Genuinely hopeful about his future, he is empowered with the freedom to make good choices. He is able to trust and receive the love of his family and friends, and this love provides a deeper sense of security than he ever remembers.

With this newfound security, John's growth in *maturity* accelerated tremendously. Since his healing experiences, he finds it much easier to practice virtuous living. He is discovering the joy of being dependent on the Father for his comfort and strength, thus replacing the ungodly self-reliance that was formed out of his wounds and inner vows. His growth in chastity has given him a deep desire to remain pure. He is more aware when the tempter brings to mind lustful images, which no longer hook into his wounds and send him into a cycle of addiction. He is able to bring these temptations into the light and does not feel compelled to act them out. John is also noticing that his desires are changing and becoming more wholesome as

Figure 11.1. Healing tree of life

FRUIT OF THE SPIRIT

PURITY

PEACE

PATIENCE

FAITHFULNESS

GENTLENESS

LOVE

GOODNESS

KINDNESS

JOY

SELF-CONTROL

SEVEN LIVELY VIRTUES
Patience *overcomes* anger
Humility *overcomes* pride
Chastity *overcomes* lust
Diligence *overcomes* sloth
Abstinence *overcomes* gluttony
Kindness *overcomes* envy
Liberality *overcomes* greed

MATURITY

ROOT OF GRACE
{COMMUNION WITH GOD}
"I will let God love me in the places
where I feel most vulnerable and
dependent."

SEVEN SIGNS OF HEALING
Connected and understood *replace* abandonment
Pure and worthy *replace* shame
SECURITY   Safe and secure *replace* fear
Empowered and liberated *replace* powerlessness
Accepted and valued *replace* rejection
Hopeful and encouraged *replace* hopelessness
Understanding and enlightenment *replace* confusion

he experiences the freedom of chastity. He is diligent in maintaining his spiritual life. Once grasping for pleasure and happiness, he is now generous with his time and possessions. He has learned to live in the Father's providence with joy. (See the trunk of the tree where lively virtues replace deadly sins.)

The fruit on John's tree feeds many around him. When we spoke, I could hear a greater *purity* of heart through everything he shared. He told me he had been free from the compulsions for several years and was deeply in love with his wife and children. Before forgiving his mother and sister, he could not love any woman. He only used them, in real life and in fantasy. Now he was capable of loving several of them (wife, mother, sister, daughter, and friends) chastely, as well as himself. He is experiencing the fruit of the Holy Spirit much more regularly in his life (see top of figure 11.1).

John and I both left our conversation over the phone with deep gratitude, praising God for what he had done. Like the woman at the well, Jesus lovingly exposed the areas of shame that kept John bound and gave him living water to drink. He is in love with Jesus and invites others to discover the same kind of freedom he enjoys.

Do you want to be healed? Do you desire the kind of freedom that John now enjoys? Is there any area of your life that you believe disqualifies you from receiving God's grace or healing? If so, your God is not big enough, and Jesus' Cross is not real enough. In one of my favorite passages of scripture, we are given this amazing promise from God: instead of your shame you will have a double portion of honor (Is 61:7). Think of the most shameful or hopeless area of your life, past or present. That is the place you most need a Savior to set you free. That same area in your life, *when* it is healed, will bring God the greatest glory in your life. For many of you, this will also be

Is there any area of your life that you believe disqualifies you from receiving God's grace or healing? If so, your God is not big enough, and Jesus' Cross is not real enough.

the very place that God will equip you to administer healing to others. Do you believe what I am saying? I know this to be true from my own personal experience and from John's. His shame was an area of his life where he most needed Jesus. Because of his healing encounters with Jesus around those issues, God is now glorified in his life through those same wounds and areas of shame.

Isn't this the promise of the Gospel? St. Paul assures us that because of Christ's redemption and the Father's providential love, "all things work for good for those who love God, who are called according to his purpose" (Rom 8:28). Look at a crucifix or an image of the crucified Jesus in your imagination. Do you believe that "we were healed by his wounds" (1 Pt 2:24)? None of his suffering is wasted or superfluous; all of it has been necessary for our salvation and healing. Now look at your own suffering and wounds and even your own sins. Can you see how every wound you have ever incurred and every sin you have ever committed, if submitted to God and redeemed, will be worked for your greater good and not just for your good? This grace extends to all the people your life touches directly and indirectly in the present and for generations to come. This confidence allows us to live with great freedom.

But notice, in Romans 8:28, freedom has a condition: that we love God and follow his calling and purpose for our life. Only when we surrender our wills and our lives to God can we find this freedom and joy. Jesus does the heavy lifting in bringing about our freedom, but we still have a part to play. Are you willing to take the next step on your journey of healing?

Continuing on Your Healing Journey

As we conclude, I want to encourage you to reflect on all we have been discussing in this book so far and apply it to your life. Consider grabbing your journal and a pen to jot down your answers.

- Have you experienced an encounter with Jesus that has transformed your life and set your heart on fire (like the woman at the well from the introduction)?
- What is your story? (See chapter 1.) Jesus is asking you if you want to be healed (as he asked the man at the pool of Bethesda). What is your response? What stands in your way? What do you want to ask him to do for you?
- What are the most important life lessons you have learned from the Good Teacher? How has God's way, truth, and life been a source of healing in your life? Which good teachers in your life have revealed Jesus to you through word and example? Have you chosen to follow Jesus as his disciple? (See chapter 2.)
- How have you experienced Jesus as the Compassionate Healer? How has he healed you personally? In what specific ways has he worked through you to bring healing to others? (See chapter 3.)
- Are you more prone to live as the "older brother" or "younger brother" (from the prodigal son story)? Have you accepted your identity as the Father's beloved son or daughter? What "identity lies" keep you bound? How have you experienced Jesus' "death therapy"? (See chapter 4.)
- What is the whole person perspective? How does it change your understanding of yourself and your brokenness? How does it affect the way you see others and their brokenness? Try applying this perspective to areas of brokenness in your life. (See chapter 5.)
- As you look at the "apples" in your life, can you see where these specific sins are rooted in your personal "tree of knowledge of good and evil"? Which of the seven deadly sins are

habitual in your life? What idols are behind these? Can you see how these developed into strongholds? (See chapter 6.)

- What responses to trauma in your life have left you bound in one or more of the seven deadly wounds? What identity lies did you internalize from the traumatic experiences? What are the judgments and inner vows that have kept you bound? (See chapter 7.)
- How has Christ's redemptive suffering been a source of healing for you personally? Give examples of how you have you entered into your own suffering in a redemptive way. What lively virtues have been cultivated in your life through your suffering? (See chapter 8.)
- What is your attitude towards the sacraments? What role do the sacraments play in your life? In what specific ways have you encountered Jesus through the sacraments? (See chapter 9.)
- How have you encountered Jesus in healing prayer? What do you think about encountering Jesus in this way? Describe an experience of prayer that resulted in one or more of the seven signs of healing. (See chapter 10.)
- Can you identify ways you are now living in freedom that were not present earlier in your life? How do you plan to maintain and increase this freedom? How are you using your freedom for the good of others and God's glory? (See this conclusion.)

Consider coming back to these questions in a few weeks, months, and years to recall how your life and perspectives have changed. I also encourage you to form a small group with a few others to share this journey of healing together. Use these questions and the questions throughout the book as a guide for your discussion.

For the greatest benefit, seek to encounter Jesus in your own individual prayer and journaling time, and then share these experiences with your trusted friends. That may come from a support group, or from finding someone who can pray for you in this way. Jesus is waiting with great anticipation. Will you meet him at the place of your thirst?

Thank you for taking this journey with me. May the Holy Spirit bring you into ever-deepening encounters with Jesus' powerful and merciful love. I pray that you may have the grace to imitate the Blessed Virgin Mary with your very own "fiat." And finally, may the Father be glorified as you come more and more fully alive in him!

ACKNOWLEDGMENTS

As I finish this section over Thanksgiving weekend, I realize how many blessings I have received in my life and in the process of writing this book. Mostly, I am grateful for God's love and mercy, expressed throughout my life and in nearly every page of this book. God is so good! I will go anywhere in the world to tell people how good he is. I pray that this book will communicate his love and goodness throughout the world and in the heart of each person who reads it.

Among my most treasured gifts in life are my family, friends, and Christian community. First I want to thank my wife, Margie and each member of our family: Carrie and Duane; Anna, Drew, Ryan, Jack, Luke, Lily, and Elle; Kristen and Stephen; Mom, Dave, and family; Kathy, Nick, and family; Lauren, Tom, and family; Wayne, Tara, and family; Bart, Brooke, and family; Margaret, Ken, and family; Dad, Paula, and family; Susan, Rich, and family; Missy, Justin, and family; Ann and Gerald; Jere, Patty, and family; Julie, Tom, and family; and Bud, Kath, and John. Thank you to my grandparents, aunts, uncles, and cousins on both sides of our large extended family. You each bring joy and fulfillment to my life. I love each of you and desire that this book will touch you in some very unique and personal way with Jesus' love.

Margie, I especially appreciate your walking this journey with me and for loving me through it all—in the good times and the hard times. Mom and Dad, thank you for your love for each of us and for

God; for never giving up hope when things were darkest; and for your humility and example in facing your own brokenness.

To the team at John Paul II Healing Center (staff, board, volunteers, and supporters), thank you for your participation in this ministry. It is a joy to share in this mission together with you. Thank you for your generosity in giving of yourselves out of love for Jesus and the people we serve. Each of you has become a treasured member of my family. I especially want to thank Bart and Ken for being sharpening tools in the Father's hands in my life during this season.

Father Mark Toups, thank you for your friendship, encouragement, and inspiration in starting our Healing the Whole Person conferences and for writing the foreword to this book. And to Bishop Sam Jacobs, thank you for being the first to entrust your seminarians to our care and for serving on our board.

To my spiritual directors, teachers, and mentors throughout the years, I thank God for the ways your love for Jesus overflows to me and my family. I offer a special thank you to Fr. Michael Foley. Thank you for giving up everything to serve our parish community for the past thirty-five years. In our family alone, you have been there at every stage of life, presiding at all the significant moments from birth to death. And, to each of the priests who have served us with Christ's love, thank you.

To all of my fellowship groups and Christian communities (Christian Therapists, Church in City, Catholic Healing Symposium, Spiritual family, and more) you are a large part of my story. Thank you for all the ways you helped form me in my quest to learn about Jesus and his healing love. To our loyal intercessors who keep us in prayer, I am grateful for your dedication in praying for this mission and in a particular way, for this book. And for the friends and supporters of our ministry, thank you for your generosity and love for God and this mission.

I thank each person whose story is represented in this book, and for the hundreds whose stories are not here, but remain written in my heart. You have each enriched my life and your healing encounters with Jesus have profoundly touched my heart.

I am also grateful to each of you who reviewed this book and gave helpful input, or offered your personal endorsements: Archbishop Samuel Aquila, Fr. Peter Ryan, Fr. John Horn, Fr. Will Ganci, Fr. Tom Dillon, Sr. Miriam James Heidland, Neal Lozano, Christopher West, Brian Butler, Jane Guenther, Gary Oates, Dr. Ray Verrier, Jill Bohacik, Jim and Lois Galbraith, Judy Bailey, Dale Recinella, Fred Thomson, Frank Voran, Joanne Arnett, Dave Schuchts, Peggy Schuchts, Ken Kniepmann, Bart Schuchts, Kathy Tafuri, Margaret Szortyka, Carrie Daunt, Duane Daunt, Kristen Blake, Wayne Schuchts, Rich Schuchts, and Margie Schuchts.

I want to offer a special thank you to Julie Bettinger for your generous help and valuable feedback over the years in coaching me as I began to write.

Finally, thank you to my editor Kristi McDonald. I thoroughly enjoyed working with you. I appreciate your strong faith, gentleness, and firm resolve. And to Bob, Susana, Jackie, Brian, and the entire team affiliated with Ave Maria Press, thank you for your wisdom and expertise in making this book what it is. You are all gifted in your craft.

NOTES

Foreword

1. The word *minister*, as it appears throughout the book, is used in a broad context to include clergy and lay persons, as well as those who serve in the name of Christ in all Christian denominations. The author acknowledges the unique role of the sacramental and ministerial priesthood, as distinct from other ministries in the Church. The lay faithful, by virtue of their baptismal call, have their own unique role in bringing the love of Christ into their particular spheres of influence, with the gifts of the Holy Spirit to aid them. See Second Vatican Council, *Gaudiem et Spes* (Church in the Modern World), for a thorough discussion of these various ministries.

2. Pope John Paul II, *Opatatium Totius*, 8 (Decree on Priestly Training); Pope Benedict XVI, *May 2006 Address to the Clergy in Warsaw Poland*.

3. Pope Benedict XVI, *May 2006 Address*.

4. Pope Benedict XVI, *Jesus of Nazareth: From the Baptism in the Jordan to the Transfiguration* (New York: Random House, 2007), 176.

5. Christopher West, *Theology of the Body Explained: A Commentary on John Paul II's "Gospel of the Body,"* rev. ed. (Boston: Pauline Books, 2003), 60.

Chapter One: Do You Want to Be Healed?

1. "Data: Indicators," World Bank, accessed September 16, 2013, http://data.worldbank.org/indicator.

2. Pope Benedict XVI, *Jesus of Nazareth*, 176.

3. A Family Reconstruction is a reenactment of one's family history, usually involving several generations. It involves role-players who stand in for family members. There is no acting involved; the people chosen to represent the family members are asked simply to assume a position and report their experience. It may sound strange, but it is an extremely powerful tool for healing deep wounds and family dynamics. If you are interested in finding out more, I would recommend Bill Nerin's book *Family Reconstruction: A Long Day's Journey into Light* (New York: Norton, 1986).

Chapter Two: The Good Teacher

1. See Henri J. M. Nouwen, *The Return of the Prodigal Son: A Meditation on Fathers, Brothers, and Sons* (New York: Doubleday, 1992); and Neal Lozano, *The Older Brother Returns: Finding a Renewed Sense of God's Love and Mercy* (Clinton Corners, NY: Attic Studio, 1995).

2. Pope Francis, *Homily on the Beatitudes during Daily Mass*, June 10, 2013.

Chapter Three: The Compassionate Healer

1. Leanne Payne, *The Healing Presence: How God's Grace Can Work in You to Bring Healing in Your Broken Places and the Joy of Living in His Love* (Westchester, IL: Crossway, 1989), 139.

2. Throughout the history of the Church, the faithful have always believed in the reality of miracles, not just in the scriptures but also in the life of believers and in certain holy places (like Lourdes). However, in the strictest sense, the Church has reserved the term *miracle* to define those supernatural interventions of God that can be validated after long and arduous investigation. In an official sense, only the Church can declare something to be a bona fide miracle. In this book, we are using the term in a broader sense, to include an apparent intervention from God that brings about a healing or other transformation of nature. None of the miracles mentioned in this book have been verified by the Church's scrutiny. However, many have been "unofficially" verified by eyewitnesses, pastors, doctors, therapists, and so forth.

3. See Pope John Paul II, *Fides et Ratio* (Faith and Reason).

4. Francis MacNutt, *Healing* (Notre Dame, IN: Ave Maria Press, 1999), 11.

5. Gary Oates, *Open My Eyes, Lord: A Practical Guide to Angelic Visitations and Heavenly Experiences* (New Kensington, PA: Whitaker, 2004).

6. Pope Francis, "Prayer Works Miracles," *L'Osservatore Romano*, no. 22, May 29, 2013.

7. Randy Clark with Global Awakening was the one leading this ministry team; see http://globalawakening.com.

8. MacNutt, *Healing*, 11.

Chapter Four: The Beloved Son

1. Peggy Papp, *The Process of Change* (New York: Guilford, 1983).

2. In his book *Unbound: A Practical Guide to Deliverance*, Neal Lozano talks about how the blessing of identity is key to our healing (Grand Rapids, MI: Chosen, 2010).

3. Pope Francis, *Homily on the Feast of the Most Sacred Heart*, Vatican Radio, June 7, 2013.

4. See Jack Frost, *Spiritual Slavery to Spiritual Sonship* (Shippensburg, PA: Destiny Image, 2006).

5. Nouwen, *Return of the Prodigal*.

6. Lozano, *Older Brother Returns*.

7. John Eldredge, *Wild at Heart* (Nashville: Thomas Nelson, 2006).

8. James Keating, "Christ Is the Sure Foundation: Priestly Human Formation Completed in and by Spiritual Formation," *Nova et Vetera* 8, no. 4 (2010): 883–99, 885.

9. Second Vatican Council, *Gaudiem et Spes* (Church in the Modern World), 22.

10. Pope Benedict XVI, *Jesus of Nazareth*, 18.

Chapter Five: The Whole Person Perspective

1. See Pope John Paul II, *Fides et Ratio* (Faith and Reason).

2. See especially part 1 of John Paul II's *Man and Woman He Created Them: A Theology of the Body*, trans. Michael W. Walstein (Boston: Pauline, 2006).

3. Pope John Paul II, *Redemptor Hominus* (Redeemer of Man), 10.

4. Pope John Paul II, *Crossing the Threshold of Hope* (New York: Knopf, 1994), 228.

5. Pope Benedict XVI, *Jesus of Nazareth*, 176.

6. International Catholic Charismatic Renewal Services (ICCRS) Doctrinal Commission, *Guidelines on Prayers for Healing*, 5th ed. (Vatican City, 2007), 37–39.

7. Centers for Disease Control and Prevention and Bruce Lipton of Stanford University Medical School, cited on home page, Healing

Codes: Heal Yourself, accessed September 18, 2013, http://www.healingcodes.com.

8. See Harold G. Koenig, Michael E. McCullough, and David B. Larson, *Handbook of Religion and Health* (Oxford: Oxford University Press, 2001); and Harold G. Koenig, *The Healing Power of Faith: How Belief and Prayer Can Help You Triumph Over Disease* (New York: Simon & Schuster, 2001).

9. J. Brennan Mullaney, *Authentic Love: Theory and Therapy* (New York: St. Pauls/Alba House, 2008), 17.

10. Ibid.

11. Pope Benedict XVI, *Jesus of Nazareth*, 177.

12. See Matthew Linn, Sheila Fabricant, and Dennis Linn, *Healing the Eight Stages of Life* (Mahwah, NJ: Paulist Press, 1988); and Erik H. Erikson, *The Life Cycle Completed* (New York: Norton, 1997).

Chapter Six: A Tree and Its Fruit

1. Pope John Paul II, *Man and Woman*, 4:1.

2. Author unknown, quoted in Stephen R. Covey, *The Seven Habits of Highly Effective People: Powerful Lessons in Personal Change* (New York: Simon & Schuster, 2004), 46.

3. Pope John Paul II, *General Audience on the Nature of Sin*, November 12, 1986.

4. See home page, 7 Deadly Sins, accessed September 19, 2013, http://deadlysins.com.

5. Adolphe Tanquerey, *The Spiritual Life: A Treatise on Ascetical and Mystical Theology*, trans. Herman Branderis (Rockford, IL: Tan Books, 2000), 392.

6. Ibid.

7. "Pride," 7 Deadly Sins, accessed September 19, 2013, http://deadlysins.com.

8. See Lozano, *Unbound*, 42–48; and Beth Moore, *Breaking Free: Making Liberty in Christ a Reality in Life* (Nashville: LifeWay, 1999), 225–28.

9. Andy Reese, *Sozo Training Manual* (Freedom Resources, 2007), 25.

10. Moore, *Breaking Free*, 226.

11. Note that depression is not always caused by suppressed anger.

12. See Blair Justice's *Who Gets Sick: Thinking and Health* (Houston: Peak Press, 1987); the American Institute of Stress (AIS) at http://www.stress.org; the American Heart Organization; the National Institute of Arthritis and Musculoskeletal and Skin Diseases; and the National Institute of Mental Health (NIMH).

Chapter Seven: Anatomy of a Wound

1. Patrick Carnes, *Contrary to Love: Helping the Sexual Addict* (Minneapolis: CompCare, 1989).

2. Russell Willingham, *Breaking Free: Understanding Sexual Addiction and the Healing Power of Jesus* (Downers Grove, IL: InterVarsity Press, 1999); Carnes, *Contrary to Love.*

3. James G. Friesen et al., *The Life Model: Living from the Heart Jesus Gave You* (Pasadena, CA: Shepherd's House, 1999), 69–70.

4. Ibid., 70–72.

5. John Wimber and Kevin Springer, *Power Healing* (New York: Harpercollins, 1987), 87–88.

6. Edward M. Smith, *Theophostic Prayer Ministry: Basic Training Seminar Manual* (Campbellsville: KY: New Creation, 2007), 104–8.

7. Ed Smith delineates two types of shame wounds—"tarnished" and "shame"—which I have combined into one category and called it "shame."

8. "Pelagius and Pelagianism," Catholic Encyclopedia, New Advent, 2009, http://www.newadvent.org/cathen/.

Chapter Eight: Redemptive Suffering

1. Pope John Paul II, *Salvifici Doloros* (On Human Suffering), 7.

2. Ibid., 19.

3. "Contrary, Heavenly, and Cardinal Virtues," 7 Deadly Sins, accessed September 19, 2013, http://deadlysins.com; Fr. Robert Barron, *Seven Deadly Sins and Lively Virtues,* Lighthouse Catholic Media, CD.

4. Pope John Paul II, *Salvifici Delores* (On Human Suffering), 19.

5. Ibid., 25.

Chapter Nine: Sacraments and Healing

1. Scott Hahn, *Swear to God: The Promise and Power of the Sacraments* (New York: Doubleday, 2004), 3.

2. Ibid.

3. Raniero Cantalamessa, *Sober Intoxication of the Spirit: Filled with the Fullness of God*, trans. Marsha Daigle-Williamson (Cincinnati: Servant Books, 2005), 61.

4. Ibid., 40–43.

5. Pope Francis, *Easter Monday Address*, April 2, 2013.

6. Pope John Paul II, *Reconciliation and Penance*, 6.

7. Ibid.

8. George Weigel, *Evangelical Catholicism: Deep Reform in the Twenty-First-Century Church* (New York: Basic, 2013), 42–43.

9. Briege McKenna, with Henry Libersat, *Miracles Do Happen* (Ann Arbor, MI: Charis, 1996), 59–61.

10. Robert DeGrandis, with Linda Shubert, *Healing through the Mass*, rev. ed. (Mineola, NY: Resurrection Press, 1992), 5.

11. Rolland and Heidi Baker, *There Is Always Enough: The Amazing Story of Rolland and Heidi Baker's Miraculous Ministry among the Poor* (Tonbridge, UK: Sovereign, 2003), 42–43.

12. Pope Benedict XVI, *Benedictus: Day by Day with Pope Benedict XVI*, ed. Peter John Cameron (San Francisco: Ignatius, 2006), 337.

13. Pope Francis, *Easter Monday Address*, April 2, 2013.

Chapter Ten: Healing Prayer

1. Pope John Paul II, *Veritatis Splendor* (Splendor of Truth), 108.

2. Pope Benedict XVI, address on Pentecost, quoted in Weigel, *Evangelical Catholicism*, 18.

3. Pope Benedict XVI, *Benedictus*, 164.

4. Cantalamessa, *Sober Intoxication*, 95.

5. Francis MacNutt, *The Power to Heal* (Notre Dame, IN: Ave Maria Press, 1992), 28.

6. Ibid., 29.

7. Ibid., 39.

8. Pope Francis, "Prayer Works Miracles."

9. Pope John Paul II, *Man and Woman*, 51:1, 326.

10. Edward M. Smith, *Healing Life's Hurts through Theophostic Prayer* (Ventura, CA: Gospel Light, 2004), 30–31; Betty Tapscott and Robert DeGrandis, *Forgiveness and Inner Healing* (Houston: Tapscott, 1980), 1.

Conclusion: Living in Freedom

1. Pope John Paul II, *Redemptor Hominus* (The Redeemer of Man), 21.

2. Second Vatican Council, *Gaudiem et Spes* (Church in the Modern World), 24.

3. Tapscott and DeGrandis, *Forgiveness and Inner Healing*, 1.

4. Pope John Paul II, *Veritatis Splendor* (Splendor of Truth), 35.

5. Tapscott and DeGrandis, *Forgiveness and Inner Healing*, 14–15.

Bob Schuchts is the bestselling author of *Be Healed, Be Transformed*, and *Be Devoted*. He is the founder of the John Paul II Healing Center in Tallahassee, Florida, and cohost of the *Restore the Glory* podcast with Jake Khym.

After receiving his doctorate in family relations from Florida State University in 1981, Schuchts became a teacher and counselor. While in private practice, he also taught graduate and undergraduate courses at Florida State and Tallahassee Community College. Schuchts later served on faculty at the Theology of the Body Institute and at the Center for Biblical Studies—where he taught courses on healing, sexuality, and marriage—and was a guest instructor for the Augustine Institute. He volunteered in parish ministry for more than thirty years.

He retired as a marriage and family therapist in December 2014.

Schuchts has two daughters and eight grandchildren. His wife, Margie, died in 2017.

jpiihealingcenter.org
www.restoretheglorypodcast.com
Twitter: @JPIIHealing
Facebook: JP2HealingCenter

MORE BOOKS BY
BOB SCHUCHTS

Be Restored
Healing our Sexual Wounds through Jesus' Merciful Love

We all have sexual wounds—some caused by over-sexualized culture, some by our personal choices, and some through the actions of others. In *Be Restored*, Bob Schuchts offers you concrete steps for healing and wholeness, relying on a combination of clinical expertise, Catholic theology, and personal experience as a survivor to guide you.

Be Transformed
The Healing Power of the Sacraments

Whether it is the wounds of past hurts, the strains in our relationships, or the stresses of daily life, we all need to be comforted and made whole by Christ. Bob Schuchts guides you to tap into the power of Christ present in the sacraments and to experience the ongoing effects of their graces in every aspect of your life.

Be Devoted
Restoring Friendship, Passion, and Communion in Your Marriage

In *Be Devoted*, Bob Schuchts presents his first resource for married and engaged couples and those who desire true love in their relationships. This guide delivers sound Catholic teaching, rich storytelling, and practical tools for healing, along with psychological insights and expertise to help couples create a relationship that is rich in trust, passion, and unity.